BAMBOO

Reaktion's Botanical series is the first of its kind, integrating horticultural and botanical writing with a broader account of the cultural and social impact of trees, plants and flowers.

Bamboo

Susanne Lucas

REAKTION BOOKS

For my father, Frank Sheridan Lucas

For the friends who inspired me to be adventurous, Marie Dolores Ianni Holland,
Toni Grieb and Ned V. Jaquith

Published by
REAKTION BOOKS LTD
33 Great Sutton Street
London EC1V 0DX, UK

www.reaktionbooks.co.uk

First published 2013
Copyright © Susanne Lucas 2013

Printed and bound in China by C&C Offset Printing Co., Ltd

A catalogue record for this book is available from the British Library

ISBN 978 1 78023 201 0

Contents

Introduction

Bamboo is thought to be the fastest growing woody plant on earth; some species can grow more than 1 metre a day. Hundreds of millions of people, animals and insects depend on it. With thousands of uses, as food, fabric, paper, shelter and inspiration, bamboo has traditionally contributed to the myriad physical requirements and spiritual needs of mankind. As the Chinese poet Su Dongpo wrote over 800 years ago, 'A meal should have meat, but a house must have bamboo. Without meat we become thin; without bamboo, we lose serenity and culture itself.'

Throughout the ages, humans have utilized bamboo; it has been cut, split, bent, dried, chopped, cooked, tied, woven, carved and crafted to help us survive and thrive. This is still true today. It is estimated that bamboo-related industries provide income, food and housing for over 2.5 billion people worldwide.[1] As a sustainable resource, bamboo may also provide potential solutions to the damaging impact of human activities on the environment. Harvesting bamboo does not kill the plant. Despite its woody appearance, bamboo is not a tree – it is a grass.

As a grass, bamboo puts out new growth in the form of stems known as 'culms'. Once the culms are cut, they are referred to as 'canes'. Bamboo culms grow to full size in a matter of a few weeks, telescoping upwards. For several years the stems do not get any larger

opposite: The bold telescoping stems (referred to as 'culms')
of *Phyllostachys atrovaginata*.

7

Photograph by Maurice Vidal Portman of a man drinking from a bamboo vessel (called *Gob-da*) in the Andaman Islands, 1890s.

The ubiquitous bamboo basket.

The beautiful new shoots of *Phyllostachys iridesens.*

in diameter, nor any taller than the height attained that first year. The bamboo survives in this way through each additional year with new shoots creating new stems, and developing a large canopy through the creation of additional branches and leaves. All the while, the roots are growing and maturing, breathing and cleaning the air, recycling water and oxygen.

Most people think they know what bamboo looks like, but in fact it occurs in many forms, including low groundcover grasses which

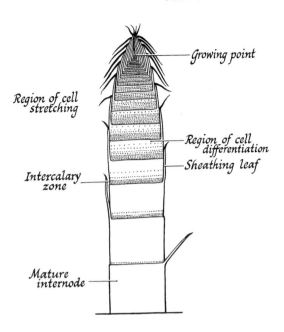

Growing point

Region of cell
stretching

Region of cell
differentiation

Sheathing leaf

Intercalary
zone

Mature
internode

The principal parts
of a typical bamboo
stem, pertaining
to how the stem
emerges, elongates
and develops.

are less than 30 cm high, and those thriving on tropical forest floors which look more like ferns than hollow-stemmed giants. The fishing-pole-style stem is a familiar bamboo image, as are tiki torches and the green leafy stems munched by giant pandas. In actuality, some bamboos are clambering vines stretching out like the tentacles of an octopus, while others bear massive thorns and create thickets. Bamboo is usually associated with the colour green, yet there exist many cultivated varieties with yellow, gold, burgundy, blue and even black stems. Some have leaves displaying an intense variegation of gold and white; some species have long, broad leaves a metre long; while others bear tiny delicate leaves in star-like tufts.

Bamboo is native to all continents except Antarctica and Europe, living in regions from sea level to the high elevations of the Himalayas,

opposite: Towering bamboo (*Phyllostachys pubescens*) forest in Kyoto, Japan.

overleaf: *Phyllostachys*, just one type of giant timber grass. The grove is comprised of a colony of individual stems, all connected below the ground in a network of rhizomes.

humid tropics, temperate cloud forests and almost-arid Indian plains. It is estimated that bamboo occupies over 39 million hectares of the world, anywhere from 4 to 10 per cent of the total forest cover in some countries.[2] In regions where bamboo no longer exists naturally, it is planted and cultivated.

Humans have shaped the landscape around them, bringing plants from the surrounding forests closer to home. The immense distribution of bamboos worldwide, the multitude of their habits and their diverse growth characteristics give this group of plants unique opportunities for fulfilling vital roles in our man-made landscapes.

Bamboo's rapid vertical growth can screen and enclose, providing privacy and protecting us from the sun and wind. It is drought and pollution tolerant. Its grove-creating rhizome root systems provide erosion control on slopes and clearings, and it develops into green woodland that is attractive to many types of bird and animal for nesting. Bamboo has the great ability to recycle carbon dioxide (an estimated up to 12 tons/hectare), cleaning the air around us – thus providing as much as 35 per cent more oxygen than the equivalent in trees.[3] Bamboo's nutritious shoots are edible and a valuable food source. It allows local harvesting for everyday needs.

Significantly, it can also be used as a substitute for timber, which is becoming scarce and relatively more expensive internationally. Bamboo forests and managed plantations can provide this valuable material if sustained properly and carefully, while protecting water-sheds and wildlife. As an agroforestry crop, bamboo has great potential for use in bioplastics, biofuels and more.

Why has the Western world not awakened to the modern potentials of bamboo? Four hundred years ago, emigrant Europeans came upon a continent where Native American peoples used the indigenous bamboo (commonly called canebrake). These canebrakes consisted of very dense, monotypic vegetation that extended across the south-eastern and lower midwestern United States, from the Mississippi River to the Atlantic coast. Within these canebrakes game animals

opposite: Close-up of the node, the cross-section of the culm.

sought shelter and food. The canebreaks also produced massive seed crops which followed cyclical flowering periods, providing food for animals and people. Local people prized the seed bounty, which they ate instead of less nutritious rice and wheat.[4] Rather than learning from the local inhabitants, the European colonists expanded traditional Old World farming practices and eventually eliminated the vast tracts of canebrake. Land clearing for the traditional agriculture favoured by the colonists and over-grazing of domesticated animals eliminated most of the native canebrakes by 1950, but some fragmented vestiges of them still exist today.[5]

Similar scenarios can be found throughout other continents. Dubbed the 'poor man's timber', bamboo was dismissed as an inferior material and replaced by supposedly more sophisticated building materials. Forests were felled to harvest more valuable woods, with little respect for the role of bamboo in these forest ecosystems, or simply to make way for human populations. Every day this phenomenon occurs around the globe.

Botanist David Fairchild was at one time manager of the Plant Introduction Program run by the U.S. Department of Agriculture. He is credited with the introduction of more than 200,000 exotic plants and varieties of established crop into the U.S. In *The World Grows Round My Door* (1947), Fairchild writes about an impressive collection of non-native bamboos growing at the United States Department of Agriculture's plant introduction station in Savannah, Georgia:

> The vast possibilities of bamboo have interested me for years . . . The one hundred and twenty-five species of bamboo growing there represent what I presume is the largest collection of these useful grasses in the world today. The meager government support that it receives reflects, perhaps, the almost universal ignorance of the Western World with regard to the possibilities of these, the largest of all the grasses.[6]

opposite: Typical bamboo workshop producing household items in Guangzhou, China.

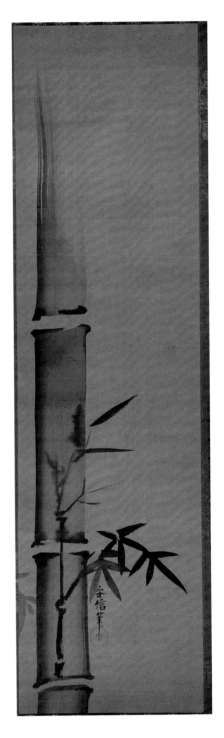

Bamboo scroll painted by
Kano Yasunobu (1613–85)
of the Kano School, Japan.

In Asia, however, bamboo has maintained a vital role. While the term 'poor man's timber' is recognized and the use of bamboo is sometimes limited to rural tribal areas (where it is an abundant natural resource), government investment in bamboo industries is on the rise. China, India, Thailand, Vietnam and the Philippines are seeing the potentials of bamboo in a modern world. Thanks to technological advances in the manufacturing of bamboo products, as well as the need to embrace sustainable forestry practices, bamboo is no longer viewed as a material used only by the poor. With the involvement of the International Network of Bamboo and Rattan, an organization headquartered in Beijing, efforts to develop government programmes focusing on bamboo are progressing.[7]

Perhaps this renewed interest in bamboo is tied to the symbolism the plant holds throughout Asia. Bamboo has such an enduring significance in China that its pictograph manifests itself in hundreds of written words, evolving within the language just as the plant has in daily use. Or perhaps it is just that, since bamboo grows so abundantly throughout the temperate and tropical regions of Asia and Africa, it makes sense for humans to continue to innovate new ways of using it. The subcontinent of India and the vast regions throughout China have enormous bamboo resources – and enormous human resources to cultivate, manage and harvest them.

In the Americas, countries such as Brazil and Colombia are also home to extensive bamboo forests. People in these regions have similarly enjoyed long histories with bamboo. But perhaps the interruption brought about by European colonization interfered with the evolution of bamboo cultivation and use. Due to industrialization and modernization in the Americas traditional materials faded away. Forested areas were cleared for more favoured crops. Human disturbance altered the ecosystems in which bamboos thrived or edged the bamboos out to marginal lands.

But bamboo was not quite forgotten. Bamboo is not the only thing that has been marginalized over the past 100 years; so have many indigenous people. Living among the bamboo, and in village-based

Like other countries in East and Southeast Asia, Burma probably made
use of lacquer articles for several centuries before the earliest dated example
in the 13th century. This water bowl was made and signed by the master
craftsman Saya Saing, 1908–11.

economies, people in rural areas or with little means have continued
to use bamboo for traditional shelter building and handicrafts. What
was once a material traded only between villages evolved into a product suitable for wider distribution and export. Small industries arose
in niche markets – for example, the use of bamboo-root segments as
handles for umbrellas, handbags and teapots. Larger industries supplied
toothpicks, chopsticks, kebab skewers, incense sticks and more. Traded
locally at first, many of these products are now widely exported to
more developed nations around the world.

In some cases, these industries have continued to grow and
thrive, as bamboo has proved to be an appropriate material for numerous products. In other cases, more contemporary materials, such as
plastics and steel, which have a longer life, have taken the place of
bamboo. This is certainly the case with baskets and crates, cages and

traps, stools and chairs. A global economy has many advantages, creating markets and development and stimulating trade, but it also shifts burdens and increases the energy consumption required by long-distance transport of goods. With the arrival of the twenty-first century, consumers with environmental consciences – with new terms and standards – have set a trend. 'Sustainable development' is a phrase that is now common in discussions about human activities and increasing population estimates. It is essentially defined as human development that meets the needs of the present without compromising the ability of future generations to meet their own needs.[8] It is often associated with the terms 'carbon footprint' and 'ecological footprint'. The latter, often abbreviated to 'footprint', expresses a measure of how much biologically productive land and water an individual, population or activity requires to produce all the resources it consumes and to absorb the waste it generates using existing technology.[9] It is usually measured in global hectares (one hectare equals approximately 2.47 acres). Because trade is global, an individual or country's footprint includes land or sea from all over the world.

Many types of bamboo are split for weaving purposes, to be used in basketry and traditional crafts.

Just one architectural style using bamboo for a roof in Ecuador.

These concerns come into play when discussing bamboo as a natural resource for use today, as a material, an alternative source of energy or a carbon sink, a natural or artificial reservoir that accumulates and stores carbon-containing compounds for an indefinite period. Carbon uptake by forestation is one method proposed for reducing net carbon dioxide emissions to the atmosphere and so limiting the extremes of climate change. It has been suggested that by protecting and managing existing bamboo forests, bamboo can be a tool for mitigating climate change.[10] This thinking is not without controversy, and further scientific research is needed to investigate whether bamboo truly excels over other plant species in its ability to capture and store carbon.

Two other terms used in contemporary dialogue regarding consumer products (or durable goods) also have their bearing on bamboo. One is 'life-cycle assessment', the commonly accepted methodology for systematically testing the environmental impact of a product, service or material.[11] The other is 'triple bottom line', which refers to the social, ecological and economic components of sustainability.[12]

An inexpensive plastic-resin chair might resist decay and elemental breakdown, but it is manufactured and distributed using fossil fuels, emits toxic chemical compounds into the air and takes many, many years to biodegrade. If bamboo is seen as a material which, through life-cycle assessment, has a lower impact on the environment (revealing an impressive triple bottom line), is shown to have high value as a carbon sink and provides other valuable products due to its sustainable forestry applications, then perhaps a bamboo chair makes more sense than a plastic one, since it is a sustainable alternative that reduces one's footprint. These are issues which will be considered when discussing the potential of bamboo later in this book.

❖

The implication here is not that bamboo will save the planet or save our souls. The intention of this book is rather to facilitate a broader understanding of bamboo, exploring its place on the planet (naturally or otherwise), its relationship with humanity and its vital connection to wildlife.

Television has brought the plight of the giant panda into every viewer's home, and since attempts to 'save the pandas' by renting them to zoos around the world attract such media attention, even small children are likely to be able tell you that the favourite food of

Snail on a variegated bamboo leaf.

the giant panda is bamboo. However, there are many other mammals, reptiles and birds, as well as insects and other invertebrates, that also need help, many of which are threatened by the same enemies as the giant panda.

Loss of habitat, encroaching human populations, loss of adequate food supply and fragmented rangelands are all destructive forces that affect these creatures as well as the bamboo in which they live. Specialized fauna have also been associated with many types of bamboo around the world, especially where large stands of woody bamboo cover (or once covered) the landscape. The specific uses of bamboo by animals include inhabiting bamboo for protection from predators or inclement weather; eating leafy bamboo vegetation, tender new shoots or abundant seed crops; and building nests with bamboo leaves, twigs and thorns. Awareness of these uses is a key part of understanding the dynamics of ecosystems and the need to conserve and protect bamboo forests.[13]

The protection and conservation of living creatures is an obligation that few human beings would dismiss. In recent times, society has worked to save trees because they are old, because they are giants or because they are sacred or historical. There are organizations established to save whales, seals and elephants. In the 1970s, the Tennessee Valley Authority in the USA was delayed in constructing hydroelectric dams, all in the name of a small fish called the 'snail darter'.[14] Moral issues abound when discussing the environment and humanity's footprint on it.

Saving our souls is one thing, but the desire to enhance our homes and gardens with beautiful plants is something most people can easily relate to. In addition to its myriad practical uses, its importance to biodiversity and its modern-day potential, bamboo is also a seductive plant. The sound of its leaves whispering in the gentlest breeze, of the giant stems knocking one other in stronger gusts, of their silent stillness after a snowfall, are just some of the many sensual aspects of this marvellous grass. With the silhouette of its leaves, the grandeur of its canopy against the sky and the cathedral-arch effect created by its magnificent stems, bamboo impresses us visually. Few plants have the capability to generate such nostalgia, reverence and, today, a fresh new perspective.

> *I repeat my vow*
> *in unchanging colors of*
> *the ageless bamboo —*
> *which still creates ten thousand*
> *generations of shadows.*
> GYOKURAN,
> *18TH CENTURY*

Oxytenanthera abyssinica in full bloom. It is the most common lowland bamboo in eastern and central Africa, and is also called savannah bamboo.

one

Distribution, Diversity and Classification

B amboo is a primitive plant, and was certainly around during the time of the dinosaurs; however, modern gene sequence models show that bamboos are more highly evolved than most grasses (diverging from close relatives such as rice, wheat and barley), arising from forests where they have adapted and filled niches.[1] Bamboos are primarily pioneers and spreaders. From fern-like manifestations on the forest floors of Costa Rica and Brazil to giant woody towers in Southeast Asia and Indonesia, bamboos have diverse habits, habitats and roles in a multitude of ecosystems. They are wind and insect pollinated, flowering annually, sporadically or rarely.

Bamboos first evolved in the tropical lowlands of what was known as Gondwanaland, between 55 and 70 million years ago. By the mid-Tertiary period, as the continental interiors became drier and more open, the terrestrial plants known as grasses began to expand into more open habitats; however, most bamboos never left the forest habitat.[2]

Contrary to the popular perception of bamboos – as giant woody trees in Asia eaten by giant pandas – bamboos thrive in diverse climate zones from sea level to above the timberline. Bamboo, as mentioned previously, is native to every continent except Antarctica and Europe, although fossil remains in Europe indicate that bamboo was once also part of that region's natural flora. DNA evidence of fossilized bamboo plant material suggests that earlier forms go back

Within the bamboo forest, looking for the sky.

26 million years.[3] On every continent where bamboo lives, there are populations of living creatures that depend on it, just like China's giant panda.

The ecological diversity of bamboo is vast. It can fill niches as creeping groundcover along the forest floor, or create vast expansive monopolies throughout mountain ranges covering thousands of acres. As a pioneer, it can be the first to arise in clearings, and it can clamber and climb atop other plants, forming lianas much like an aggressive vine. The distribution of bamboos globally is governed largely by rainfall, temperature, altitude and soil. Climatically bamboo prefers regions of high rainfall, ranging from about 1,200–6,300 mm or even more; though it also occurs in dry deciduous forests with rainfall as low as 750 mm. The distribution of various bamboos in areas adjoining seacoasts appears to be governed to a great extent by the relative humidity. And in terms of light, there are bamboos that demand high intensity, as well as those that require an overhead canopy for protection.[4]

Just as the variety of bamboos is extensive, so are the habitats in which they thrive. Bamboo grows in a wide variety of soil types, derived from different parent rocks within its climatic habitat. Most often, each species of bamboo has its own optimum site within an ecosystem, and different bamboo species rarely occur in combination or close association. Bamboos can make luxuriant growth on hillsides and on well-drained sandy loam to loamy soils, providing adequate nutrients and moisture are available. Soil moisture plays an important role in the distribution of various bamboo species, greatly affecting the regeneration and clump size of bamboos. Bamboos are conspicuously absent on extremely acid, saline and alkali soils, preferring acidic to near neutral pH. There are some bamboos that can tolerate clay soils and even quite moist situations such as riverbanks, while some bamboos can survive climatic conditions typifying xerophytic characteristics.[5] In such cases, special evolutionary morphological adaptations identified as air canals in the part of the roots called rhizomes (which are essentially underground stems that serve root-like functions and bear the buds from which the actual roots originate) allow for such specific niches.[6]

Bamboos seldom exist in pure monocultures but are generally found as an understorey to tree species or in mixed grasslands. Some

Bamboo often grows in mixed forest, not total monocultures.

species are confined to small forest areas (less than 100 square hectares), while others are distributed throughout vast forests of more than 2 million square hectares. In Asia alone, it is estimated that over 6.3 million square hectares potentially contain bamboo.[7]

The iconic image of bamboo as a vertical skyscraper with hollow stems really relates to just a few genera. Those images from the South Pacific or of the forests in China are indeed of bamboos – what are called 'timber bamboo' – but there are many more types of bamboo, which occurs in all shapes and sizes. If you came across bamboos while hiking in subtropical regions of South America, or along the slopes of volcanoes, you probably would not recognize them as such. Grassy tufts, entire pastures and tangled briar patches might all turn out to be bamboo species. In northern South America, especially in Colombia and Ecuador, the 'guadual' dense bamboo forest dominated by *Guadua angustifolia* is an important vegetation type at low and mid-altitude.[8] The bamboo-dominated areas of the Amazon region occupy between 121,000 and 180,000 square kilometres,[9] and can often be impenetrable because of the thorns present on some species.

Yes, bamboo has flowers. *Chusquea* in bloom.

The soft, graceful texture of the leaves of moso, *Phyllostachys pubescens*.

Pure stands of bamboo do exist, and in some cases there are cultivated regions of bamboo plantation that have been managed for hundreds of years, as seen extensively in the province of Zhejiang, China. In other areas, woody bamboos have become invasive and dominate forest succession in abandoned cultivation, excluding regeneration of native tree species.[10]

The giant timber bamboos are indeed quite impressive. Each year, massive sprouts (called 'shoots') emerge from an extensive underground root system. The diameter of the sprouts correlates to the same diameter of the mature stem (the 'culm'), meaning that it comes out of the ground and shoots to the sky, like a periscope, in just a few weeks' time. If the ultimate height of this culm is 40 metres, it achieves this in just that first growing season, never getting any taller in height or larger in diameter. This has lead to the claim that 'you can watch it grow', with some species growing over 1 metre a day. Temperate 'woody' bamboos in prime climate zones and the giant tropical bamboos growing throughout Southeast Asia reach great heights very quickly, within weeks of sprouting from the soil. The rest of that

Dendrocalamus asper is a very valuable species for human utilization, both as timber and as food.

individual culm's life span is spent in making additional branches, leaves and roots, expanding itself like a family, a colony; it does not get any taller or broader, as true trees do. The individual culm's root expansion leads to the formation of new generations of shoots, and over a period of time (anywhere from eight to ten years) the individual declines and dies, leaving behind younger culms to bring forth future culms.

Bamboos have a wide natural distribution, occurring from approximately 46°N latitude to 47°S latitude and from sea level to as much as 4,300 metres (*c.* 14,000 feet) in elevation in equatorial highlands.[11] Atlantic forests of Brazil, montane cloud forests in China, humid lowland tropics of Indonesia, tropical dry habitats in the Himalayas, vast temperate zones in Japan and Korea, subalpine Chile, alluvial plains of North America: these are all homelands for bamboo.

There exist small, almost fern-like bamboos, referred to as 'herbaceous', which have little or no woody tissue. These herbaceous bamboos (tribe Olyreae, see Map 1) are concentrated in the Neotropics, where twenty genera and approximately 110 species are found, from Mexico to northern Argentina, Paraguay and southern Brazil as well as in the West Indies.[12] *Buergersiochloa*, which includes only one species, is endemic to New Guinea.[13] Members of this tribe rarely occur above 1,000 metres in elevation. One of the neotropical species, *Olyra latifolia*, is somewhat weedy and, unsurprisingly, it is the most widely distributed herbaceous bamboo, known from tropical Africa and Madagascar in addition to its broad neotropical distribution. *O. latifolia* is clearly naturalized in tropical Africa and Madagascar, but the question of whether it is truly native to these areas is still debated. We have used a lighter shade of gold to indicate this uncertainty.[14]

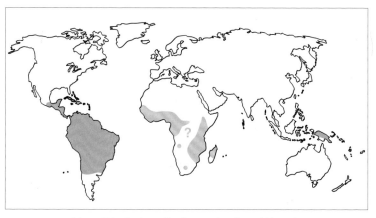

Map 1: Distribution of herbaceous bamboos (Olyreae).

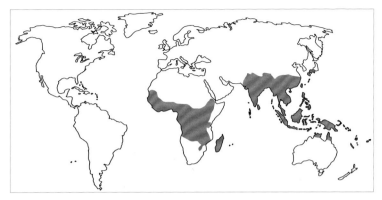

Map 2: Distribution of all woody bamboos (Bambuseae).

The woody bamboos (the most recognizable as 'bamboo', see Map 2) are much more widely distributed, both geographically and altitudinally, than the herbaceous bamboos.[15]

Within the woody bamboos, there are three major groups: the paleotropical woody bamboos, the neotropical woody bamboos and the north temperate woody bamboos. The paleotropical bamboos (Map 3) are distributed in tropical and subtropical regions of Africa, Madagascar, India, Sri Lanka, Southeast Asia, southern China, southern Japan and Oceania.[16]

The neotropical bamboos are distributed from Mexico south to Argentina and Chile and in the West Indies. The north temperate woody bamboos are widespread and diverse in the North Temperate

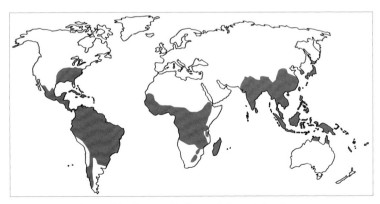

Map 3: Distribution of paleotropical woody bamboos.

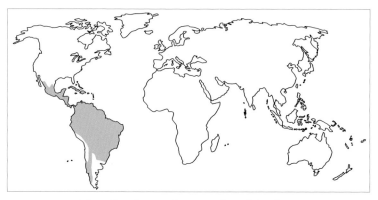

Map 4: Distribution of neotropical woody bamboos.

Zone but some members occur at higher elevations in parts of Africa, Madagascar, southern India, Sri Lanka and Southeast Asia.[17]

Nearly half of the world's 1,200 species are native to North and South America and the Caribbean. These are also more diverse than their Asian counterparts, recognized scientifically only in the last few decades.[18]

Carl Linnaeus is credited with the classification system used to give plants their names. In 1753, *Species Plantarum* was published; it outlined the principles of taxonomic nomenclature that led to the classification of plants. The system relies on the study of flower parts and remains the starting point of plant nomenclature as it exists today.

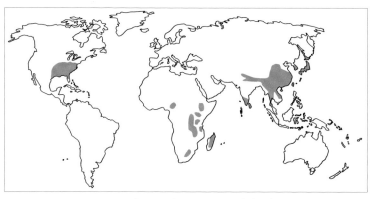

Map 5: Distribution of temperate woody bamboos.

Clumps of native *Chusquea* in the grasslands of Chile.

It is common knowledge that plants flower; however, some flowers are obscure while others are attractive. Bamboo flowers can be thought of as obscure, but can also be considered phenomenal, because some bamboos rarely flower (for example, only once every 60 years), and also because sometimes when a certain bamboo flowers, it means death for the mother plant. Bamboos are superior in evolutionary terms due to the fact that they do not rely solely on flowering for reproduction. Reproduction occurs primarily through vegetative propagation, through rhizomes, roots and new culms. Young plants grown from seed can be quite vulnerable to nature, and therefore this form of reproduction is not considered a strong evolutionary trait.

Most non-woody herbaceous bamboos flower annually, much like the roadside grasses you might swish by in the late summer. But many woody bamboos display unusual flowering cycles barely understood by science. Because of this, an explanation as to why some bamboos flower so infrequently will not be found in this book. Yet it is amazing that some of these bamboos exhibit what is called 'gregarious monocarpy', meaning that an entire stand of bamboo will begin to flower, stop making leaves or new shoots, put all its energy into producing seed and then die. 'Monocarpy' means one seed: the bamboo makes only one crop of seeds in its life, then dies. What rules dictate the death of the parents for the survival of the seedlings? Nature is full of such questions.

What happens to the local ecology when a bamboo species dies after flowering at the end of a long vegetative period of growth? Such an event has catastrophic economic and social consequences (because

An intricate flower full of pollen of monocarpic *Fargesia murieliae*.

of the suddenness and scale). It has a major impact on the local ecosystem, affecting the vegetation and wildlife with which it is associated, and it increases the possibility of soil erosion, as well as having a detrimental impact on the local population, creating food insecurity. The latter is mostly due to the sudden shortage of its nutritious seeds and fruits, which field rats feed on. Without this resource, the ferocious rats search out more food and, if humans are living nearby, raid household grain stocks. In Mizoram, in the northeastern part of India, a revolution was sparked as a result. In Thailand, the flowering of *Dendrocalamus asper* brought a flourishing edible shoots export industry to its knees. In Zambia, whole communities were uprooted when the bamboo mainstay of their lives and livelihoods flowered and died. Chaos can ensue from the death of the local bamboo.[19]

The natural regeneration, or recolonization, of bamboos occurs profusely after each mass flowering. It takes time, but after about six years, the region is again naturally populated with bamboo.[20]

It is believed that bamboo originally existed only in the monopodial form (with extensive, running root systems), which continues growing throughout the year, with periods of rhizome growth alternating with those in which new shoots and culms develop (also dependent on soil temperatures). In the tropics, however, where the rainy season is followed by long drought, lack of water makes such growth patterns impossible. It is probably as a consequence of this that the sympodial form (with non-spreading, clumping roots) developed. In this form, the rhizome and culm have essentially become one, so that the bamboo can accomplish all its growth during the rainy season, then rest during the remainder of the year.[21]

The ecological role of bamboo in forests is essentially multi-faceted. Bamboos naturally grow as a component of forests; some species as low-growing groundcovers, some as a part of the understorey and others as the woody 'trees'. Their roles vary depending on what type of forest they inhabit, but there is good evidence that shows that where bamboo lives, there is a reduction in soil erosion.[22]

Bamboo also appears to play a role in the protection and regeneration of forests. Detailed studies in Asiatic old-growth forests that have a bamboo understorey show the influence of the life cycle of the bamboos on the age structure of tree populations, and the tendency of synchronization of tree regeneration following bamboo dieback due to mass flowering.[23]

In Costa Rica, oak forest regeneration surges as a consequence of the synchronous life cycle of the *Chusquea* bamboos due to mass flowering. The *Chusquea* bamboo normally grows as the understorey in the oak forests. In the steady state, the understorey *Chusquea* clumps are small because of limited light conditions. If there are fires or gap creation through trees that fall, the *Chusquea* rapidly responds to the increased availability of light, and grows up to become the local dominant species with a closed canopy. In this situation, the young tree saplings grow in a suppressed state because of the low light conditions under the bamboo canopy. When the *Chusquea* flowers gregariously and dies, the forest floor is more illuminated, and the already established suppressed saplings shoot up. The new generation of bamboo then grows under the newly formed tree canopy.[24] Bamboos are also capable of colonizing disturbed lands. Because of its well-developed underground root systems, bamboo easily colonizes areas after outbreaks of fire. The widespread distribution of *Melocanna baccifera* (locally known as 'muli') throughout eastern India, Bangladesh and Thailand, and species of *Thyrsostachys* in Thailand and *Schizostachyum* in Vietnam, mainly occurs as secondary vegetation due to the destruction of tropical rainforest by fire, shifting cultivation and logging.[25]

Back to that great naturalist, Linnaeus. In his *Species Plantarum*, he referred to bamboo as *Arundo bambos*. However, early references to the plants now known as 'bamboo' appeared in writing long before that. The first mention of bamboo in Western literature was made in a letter from Alexander the Great to Aristotle. Later, in the early part of the seventeenth century, botanist Caspar Bauhin of Basel, Switzerland, used the name *Arundo arbor* to describe the woody, tree-like reeds he collected in India. His book, commonly known as *Pinax*, appeared in 1623; in it he also uses the term 'Bambus', which is later adopted by Linnaeus as the basis of his *Arundo bambus* in 1753, and from which the genus name of *Bambusa* was later adapted. So begins the long journey of bamboo nomenclature and its scientific classification.[26]

Superior techniques of identification and classification, such as modern DNA sequencing and genetic fingerprinting, are increasingly resolving some of the confusion clouding bamboo classification.[27] New discoveries are leading to continued reorganization of bamboo phylogeny and bamboo names.

Bamboo fits into various categories. First, it is an angiosperm, a name used to describe any plant that flowers, has an endosperm within the seeds and produces fruits that contain seeds. Flowering plants that are not angiosperms are called gymnosperms and include conifers, cycads and *Ginkgo*. Algae, mosses and ferns are more primitive non-flowering plants. Bamboo is also a monocotyledon: a flowering plant that typically has one seed-leaf (cotyledon) instead of two when the seed first sprouts. Bamboos have a single sprout at the beginning, straight up, like a blade of grass. Bamboos are in the subclass Commelinid, which separates out some of the monocotyledons. It includes several orders of plants: palms (Arecales); spiderwort and water hyacinth (Commelinales); grasses (including bamboo), rushes, rice, wheat, maize, sugar cane, pineapple and other bromeliads (Poales); ginger and banana (Zingiberales). *Poales* are flowering plants that usually have fairly small flowers, enclosed in a bract (a leaf-like piece at the base of the flower) and shaped into a cluster (inflorescence). Most plants in this order have seeds that contain starch. Many of the plants in this group are wind pollinated.[28]

Poaceae is the name of the family of plants that are most often simply called grasses. Many of the plants are staple food producers: wheat, barley, oats, rice, wild rice, corn (maize), sorghum, sugar cane and millet. Characteristic of this family are hollow stems (culms) plugged with nodes at intervals, alternate leaves with parallel veins and leaves consisting of a lower sheath and a blade. A fringe of hairs (the ligule) forms at the junction between the sheath and the blade. The flowers form into spikelets. They are hermaphroditic (male and female parts are not in separate flowers, except in corn). The fruit (seed) is called a 'caryopsis', which has the seed coat fused to the fruit wall. The bamboo family includes twelve subfamilies, one of which is Bambusoideae (see Appendix 1).

In the Bambusoideae, the flowers have three stigmas (the stigma is the part of the pistil that receives the pollen). Within the bamboos there are woody bamboos and herbaceous bamboos. The herbaceous ones seem to be trickier to define than the woody ones. The woody ones are almost tree-like. Botanists once considered the plants in

A close-up image shows the intricate morphology of bamboo shoots often used for proper identification of a species. This is *Phyllostachys nigra*.

Bamboo and mantis, woodblock print from the *Mustard Seed Garden Manual*, from China, made during the Qing Dynasty, *c.* 1701. The images are complemented by poems in fine calligraphy and the seals of the artists.

this subfamily primitive among the grass family; however, there is considerable new evidence that the bamboos are a major lineage of grasses that form part of the main diversification of the family and as such are not primitive. It is fair to say that the bamboos (Bambusoideae) are the only lineage of grasses to diversify mainly in forest habitats.[29]

So, that iconic image of bamboo – tall, segmented stems like a fishing pole – is really only representative of a few genera (for example *Phyllostachys, Dendrocalamus, Bambusa*), which have been utilized by human cultures in thousands of ways. Bamboo's multitude of forms, habits, sizes, colours, branching patterns, leaf patterns and flowers is remarkable and no doubt contributes to the general misunderstanding of this immense group of plants.

The point here is that bamboo is not just one kind of plant; it is a large group of plants that display amazing diversity. While most people living in the northern and western hemisphere think of bamboo as an Asian plant, it is Asian, American, African, Indian, Brazilian and much more. It is a plant that is ancient, but has evolved and adapted and remains vital to many natural and man-made environments around the world.

Classical woodblock print by Japanese artist Isoda Koryusai depicting the digging of moso bamboo shoots in snowy ground, *c.* 1760–80.

two

Horticulture

For centuries, humans have been searching for plants from outside their habitats to provide solutions to everyday problems and to enhance their well-being. Plant pioneers went out in search of botanical candidates to bring back for cultivation as a food source and for purely aesthetic reasons. Consequently the basic cultivation of plants led to the evolution of horticulture.

In Asian gardens, bamboo easily secured an important position due to its powerful symbolism and spiritual significance, and its practical use in all kinds of day-to-day items, for example as a building material and food source. It is no surprise that bamboo is found cultivated throughout villages for local use and outside temples in reverence of its symbolic associations.

Bamboo use in modern horticulture has been widely documented ever since early plant collectors of the Victorian era brought plants to Britain and other parts of Europe from far-off places like China, Japan and Chile. In 1868, William Munro's *A Monograph of the Bambusaceae* published by the Linnean Society of London brought scientific attention to these plants, but it was the publication in 1896 of *The Bamboo Garden* by A. B. Freeman-Mitford that brought these exotic plants into fashion throughout the British Isles.

Freeman-Mitford opens his book with this eloquent introduction:

If there be one feature which more than any other distinguishes our modern gardens from the trim pleasaunces

Bamboo ink painting on paper by Hidaka Tetsuo from 1855,
during the Edo Period, Japan.

[pleasure gardens] in which our forebears took their ease,
playing their rubber of bowls decorously on lawns hemmed in
by Yew hedges as stiff as their own ruffs, it is the value given
to beauty of form in plants as apart from that of colour. No one
who has seen at their best the giants and pigmies of the Bamboo
family will deny their supreme loveliness in this respect.

He goes on to describe the many garden varieties of bamboo introduced into England in the nineteenth century; however, even at that
time, the confusion over naming in the bamboo world was already felt
and discussed extensively.

Across the globe, Wilhelm Sulpiz Kurz, a young German who had
been curator of the Royal Botanical Garden herbarium in Calcutta
but had left for Indonesia to study bamboo, published a paper, 'Bamboo
and its Use' (1876). Unfortunately Kurz died before finishing his
account of bamboos in India, but James Sykes Gamble later used his
observations, notes and specimens for his monograph on the bamboos
of British India. Gamble was born in London and educated in France,
and served as director of the Imperial Forest School at Dehra Dun in
India for almost ten years, from 1890 to 1899.[1]

Towards the end of the nineteenth century, an Englishman, Sir
Ernest Satow, published a book that was essentially a translation of a

Archive photograph from W. E. Linscomb and the Vermilion Historical Society showing one Dr C. J. Edwards in his bamboo grove, stating it is 60 ft high and 7 in in diameter, at Abbeville, Louisiana, *c.* 1902.

Historic photograph by Michael Maslan of two men walking along a road
through an old bamboo grove in Japan, 1890s.

Japanese work by Katayama Nawohito, *Nihon Chiku-Fu* (1885). Satow's
book, *The Cultivation of Bamboos in Japan*, published by the Asiatic Society
of Japan in 1899, provided Latin names for the various species, but
most were invalid according to the stringent codes set out by the institutions overseeing botanical nomenclature in those days. What is
extremely helpful in this book is the Japanese terms for the bamboos,
which fortunately have remained the same over centuries.[2]

Proper naming of bamboos was, and still is, a difficult process.
Nomenclature of plants is based on flower parts (the Linnaean system);
however, most bamboos flower infrequently at best. Because of this,
the literature concerning horticulturally significant bamboos throughout the past 400 years shows a contradictory array of names.

In 1878, Sir Dietrich Brandis of Germany, working with the British
on forestry matters in Burma and India, established the Imperial Forest
School, and later published a remarkable paper (considering he did

opposite: The bizarre compressed nodes of tropical bamboo *Bambusa vulgaris* 'Wamin'.

Phyllostachys grove in L'Orto Botanico di Roma.

not work principally on bamboo) in 1907 on the structure and form of bamboo leaves, leading to progress in the classification and further understanding of bamboos.[3]

Along with Satow, Adrien Franchet, a botanist at the Muséum National d'Histoire Naturelle in Paris, produced publications on various bamboos in the late 1880s. Franchet is responsible for describing

some very interesting woody bamboos – the curious *Glaziophyton* from Brazil, which he named in honour of the French landscaper and botanist from Rio de Janeiro, M. Glaziou, in 1889, and *Fargesia*, named for the French missionary in the Sichuan province of China, Abbé Farges, in 1893.[4]

In 1906, Jean Houzeau De Lehaie, a Belgian, began writing a periodical bulletin titled *Le Bambou Son Etude, Sa Culture, Son Emploi*. He states:

> Our aim is the felicity for botanists and lovers of Bamboo . . . to let better know the horticultural value of these plants and, giving information on the process of culture and on places they can be obtained, to spread as much as possible their use in parks and gardens.

Written in the French language, this was no doubt a great resource for those eager to plant bamboo in appropriate climates throughout Europe, and was followed by another French work: *Les Bambusées: Monographie, Biologie, Culture, Principaux Usages* (1912) by E. G. Camus. Although these publications revolved mostly around the use of bamboo in gardens, their authors frequently commented on the remarkable diversity of species and their suitability for a variety of uses that would benefit society and the environment.

Collecting, trading and propagation of bamboos continued across Europe and the U.S. In August 1961, the United States Department of Agriculture printed *Growing Ornamental Bamboo* by Robert A. Young and J. R. Huan (USDA Bulletin No. 76). This small booklet describes

Earthenware plate depicting the newly fashionable bamboo,
made by the French artist Joseph Laurant Bouvier in 1869.

Asian-origin bamboos for garden use, following an incredible phase
of importation of bamboos into the U.S. from China, Japan and
Korea. The intention of the importations at the time was to investigate wood substitutes as sources for paper pulp, as well as other
opportunities for domestic use. However, despite intensive research
and positive results, the industrialization of bamboo never took hold
in the U.S.

Around the same time, Argentine grass specialist Professor Lorenzo
R. Parodi defined the subfamily Bambusoideae while researching samples from his country, placing all the woody bamboos in the
tribe Bambuseae. Meanwhile, a vital publication in English, *Studies
on the Physiology of Bamboo*, appeared out of Japan – the research of
Koichiro Ueda, an authority on bamboo study and professor at Kyoto

University.[5] This book revealed unknown aspects of bamboo physiology, particularly in relation to how bamboo grows, its flowering and applied studies on its cultivation and use. It stands today as a very significant contribution to the understanding of bamboo botanically and horticulturally.

Only a few years later, in 1966, an extremely valuable text appeared. This was *The Bamboos: A Fresh Perspective* by Floyd Alonzo McClure. McClure was an American who encountered bamboo as a biology school teacher in China, where he also served as an agricultural explorer for the USDA. He was surrounded by bamboo in China, and as early as 1934 had studied the morphology of a flower spikelet of a bamboo called *Schizostachyum*. He later worked at the Smithsonian Institution in the U.S., where his plan was to revise all of the bamboo genera for *Die Natürlichen Pflanzenfamilien* (the monumental German treatise, *The Natural Plant Families*). Unfortunately, at the time of his death in 1970, he had not completed the project, having only got as far as the New World bamboos. McClure dedicated his life to studying every aspect of bamboo – botanically and horticulturally – and *The Bamboos: A Fresh Perspective* was a very comprehensive work.[6] It was reprinted in 1993, and is still widely regarded as a bamboo 'bible' today.

Bamboos, by Alexander H. Lawson, the first British book devoted entirely to bamboo since Freeman-Mitford's in 1896, appeared over 70 years later in 1968. It was the first book of its kind to deal purely with temperate (cold-hardy) bamboo; the cultivation and propagation of bamboos and their potential in garden settings are discussed extensively. It was exactly the book that so many gardeners and plant enthusiasts needed to dispel the myths and help them gain confidence in using these remarkable plants effectively in modern landscapes.

Bamboo was finding its niche as a plant with unique qualities and enduring attributes in a variety of settings, from respected horticultural institutions such as Kew, Wakehurst and Wisley, to small plots and

overleaf: Bamboo can make an intriguing maze for garden whimsy and delight. Clumping bamboo, *Bambusa multiplex*, is a perfect choice.

Bamboos with beautiful stripes of colour are desirable ornamental plants for garden use.

private gardens. Gardeners who were keen to have an exotic collection of newly introduced plants welcomed bamboo as they did many other foreign imports. The great valley gardens of Cornwall are testament to this phenomenon, dating back to the turn of the twentieth century. In harsher climates, bamboo created an exotic atmosphere, growing rapidly and remaining green regardless of cold winters. Many types of bamboo exhibit colourful stems and brightly variegated leaves, a perfect foil for formal evergreens. Some species will quickly create screens and hedges, while low-growing groundcovers will spread down slopes difficult to maintain with traditional turf grasses and prevent erosion.

In 1855, in Cévennes, France, a man named Eugene Mazel set out to fulfil his dream of creating a bamboo plantation, a *bambouseraie*. The natural conditions of the site and local microclimate proved very favourable, and after constructing extensive waterworks to draw the required irrigation from the river Gardon, Mazel achieved his aim. Unsurprisingly, he also spent a lot of money, and in 1902 the plantation was sold to Gaston Nègre, who devoted a great deal of energy to restoring and enriching Mazel's collections. Today the botanical park comprises a thriving collection of plants, fabulous gardens, extensive bamboo groves (some over 25 metres tall), a bamboo labyrinth and retail outlets. The *bambouseraie* has become a mecca for people seeking the splendour of bamboo.[7]

Documentation of the various kinds of bamboo able to tolerate cold climates in countries like Germany, Denmark, the Netherlands and the northeastern parts of the United States stimulated the curiosity of plant enthusiasts. The 'tropical' appeal of bamboo made it an attractive addition to the typical plant palette found in most gardens. In 1979, the American Bamboo Society (ABS) was formed in the United States,[8] bringing together bamboophiles for the purpose of education and networking. Plant sales and auctions sponsored by the ABS expanded the cultivation and propagation of rarely seen bamboos, while the publication of a newsletter and scientific journal aided the spread of knowledge. In 1984, self-proclaimed 'bambusero' David Farrelly published an imaginative text, *The Book of Bamboo*, which prompted another surge in bamboo fervour. This acclaimed book still elicits enthusiastic reactions from beginners and experts alike, through its poetic approach to the subject.

There are many very cold-hardy bamboos for northern climates, originating in higher elevations of China. This is a bamboo of the genus *Fargesia*.

Thanks to innovative European nursery entrepreneurs who marketed bamboo plants in the 1980s to an eager public, various groups also formed in Europe, leading to the foundation of the European Bamboo Society. Belgium, the Netherlands, Germany, Switzerland, Italy, France and the United Kingdom all have individually managed membership groups focused on the cultivation of bamboo. Regional meetings, garden tours and plant sales are part of the camaraderie that keeps these bamboo enthusiasts together. The early 1990s saw the rise of international coordination between these groups, leading to the formation of the World Bamboo Organization (WBO).[9] Formally set up as a United States trade association, the mission of the WBO is simple: to encourage and promote the sustainable cultivation and use of bamboo globally. Every three years the organization holds the World Bamboo Congress in an effort to expand the networking and collaboration of international bamboo researchers, producers, institutions, artisans, architects, developers and other enthusiasts.

In order to grow bamboo, even at an amateur level, basic horticultural knowledge is essential. The sheer variety of types can quickly overwhelm those with only a casual interest in them. Bamboo comprises a large group of plants and there are distinct differences between the various categories. Bamboo types are often divided into 'tropical' and 'temperate', denoting the climates in which each kind thrives. Another broad distinction relates to the root system of bamboos – the designations 'clumping' and 'running'. 'Clumping' bamboos are those that possess pachymorph (short, thick) roots, while 'running' bamboos have leptomorph (long, thin) root systems. For the home gardener, it is important to select the appropriate type of bamboo based on its intended function. This might be to provide shade and protection from strong winds, to be a focal point as a bold specimen or to act as low-maintenance groundcover.

In addition to deciding what kind of bamboo to grow, a gardener will need to know how to plant bamboos and how to care for them. This requires information about adequate irrigation, fertilization, maintenance and successful propagation techniques. Most of these

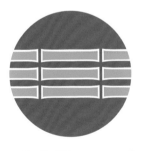

World Bamboo

The official logo of the World Bamboo Organization, dedicated to promoting the sustainable development of bamboo. Logo design by Karl Stier of Watershed Media.

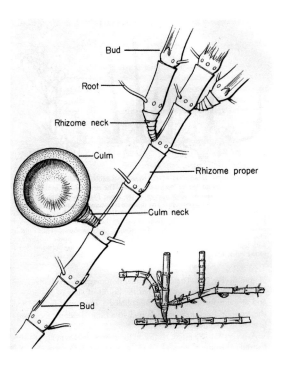

F. A. McClure's illustration of the monopodial rhizome root system of lepto-morph bamboos.

Bud

Root

Rhizome neck

Culm

Rhizome proper

Culm neck

Bud

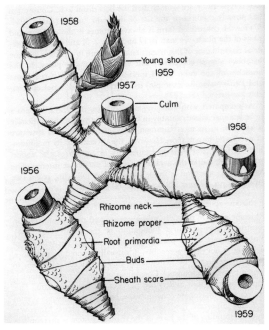

1958

Young shoot 1959

1957

Culm

1958

1956

Rhizome neck

Rhizome proper

Root primordia

Buds

Sheath scars

1959

F. A. McClure's illustration of the sympodial rhizome root system of pachymorph bamboos.

issues are dependent on which bamboo is selected and the gardener's particular climate zone.

It is not unusual to find bamboo thriving in gardens outside of its natural habitat. Most garden plants originated elsewhere, emigrating and naturalizing, becoming 'typical' in man-made landscapes as they fulfilled a practical need or aesthetic desire. Many bamboos have spread far and wide from their original habitats due to their commercial value, based on their specific characteristics. It is difficult to track down the origin of certain bamboos since, having been cultivated for centuries, they sometimes appear to be native to their adopted landscapes.

Like other garden plants originating in China, Japan, South America and South Africa – such as forsythia, azalea, poinsettia and gerbera daisy – bamboos have been found to be a desirable (and indeed fashionable) component in contemporary garden design.

Some species of plant from 'exotic' locations can become troublesome, spreading seed far and wide and invading spaces where they were not intended to grow. These plants are sometimes referred to as 'invasives'. However, cultivated bamboos rarely flower or seed, and do not jump spatial boundaries. Of course, bamboo types with running rhizomes can be amazingly aggressive and 'invade' land, but careful maintanence by responsible gardeners can keep bamboo in its place. The clumping, non-invasive bamboos are better choices for the home landscape if space or maintenance opportunities are limited. Neglected bamboo will certainly become problematic and in such circumstances, the appeal and merits of the plant will be lost.

Garden books focusing on the horticultural aspects of bamboo deal with appropriate species, hardiness, cultural details, maintenance requirements, how to control running types and so on, and are listed in the bibliography. Due to the vast number of genera and species, regional conditions dictate which bamboos can thrive where, so the gardener will learn not only from reading, but also through trial and error. One might be advised that bamboos are best planted in the winter, but this only applies to places such as the West Coast of the

A plantation of *Phyllostachys pubescens* in Portugal.

United States where rainfall is usual; for regions where below-freezing temperatures are the norm, the correct advice would be to plant in spring. Depending on the species, one may annually harvest an exotic tasty treat for human consumption, or fodder to donate to local zoos. Much depends on the local climate, type of bamboo, hemisphere and other regional characteristics.

three

The Hand of Man

There is compelling evidence to suggest that the first books were made of bamboo. Early man wrote on cave walls and stone surfaces, and later on bone and tortoise shells, but it is thought that books themselves were made of bamboo. In China, the earliest surviving examples date from the fifth century BC, but it is believed that bamboo strips were in use as early as 1250 BC in the late Shang period.[1] These long, narrow strips of bamboo were one of the main tools for literacy in early China, and subsequently in medieval Japan. Each page would typically carry a single column of brush-written text, with space for additional Chinese characters, and the strips of bamboo would be connected with string binding.

Bamboo books varied in size and shape, sometimes depending on the information conveyed in the text. Bamboo was chosen as a writing material over wood because of its unique properties and sheer abundance within China. Bamboo is lightweight, easily split into sections and has a durable surface. Once cut into appropriate widths and lengths, the epidermis of green skin was scraped off and cured by heat. The process of making bamboo into writing tablets was called *sha-ch'ing*, as described by bibliographer Lin-Hsiang (*c.* 80–8 BC).[2]

The split pieces were aligned vertically, with a single line of characters written on them running from top to bottom. It is thought that originally the strips were written on before binding, but later, with

opposite: Bamboo provided an ideal material for the first books, dating back to the 5th century BC.

The split stems of early books contained the text and were easily rolled, then tied with twine for easy transport.

longer texts, it became more practical for the strips to be bound first. The books would be rolled up, starting with the left-hand side and rolling to the left, so that the last page would be at the centre, the first page on the outside. The method of writing vertically and reading from left to right was retained when books started to be printed on paper in the seventh century AD.[3]

The use of bamboo as a writing material has a much longer history than paper. Silk was also used, and overlapped with bamboo for over 1,000 years. Paper eventually began to displace bamboo in mainstream use, and by the fourth century AD bamboo was largely abandoned when the self-appointed emperor of Chu ordered that paper should be used instead of bamboo strips.[4]

Paper has been made from bamboo for over 1,000 years in China.

In addition to being used to write upon, bamboo became an instrument for writing. In ancient China writing evolved into a kind of art, and most often writing brushes were made of bamboo. Not surprisingly, the written characters of the Chinese and Japanese languages include bamboo pictographs. When such characters began to be developed some four million years ago, the pictographs drew from everyday life. The Japanese kanji for bamboo, 竹 (*take*), shows two stalks topped with spiky leaves. A component in over 165 kanji characters, 竹 is a physical part of the Japanese language.[5] The vertical lines of 竹 are abbreviated so they can be written in the top position, where they are always found. The symbol for the writing brush, 筆 (*fude*), has for over 2,000 years included the character for bamboo. Similarly, 算 (*san*, meaning 'calculate')

Traditional
calligraphy master
Cho-am in Damyang,
South Korea.

is topped with bamboo, indicating the material used to make what
looks to be a rectangular abacus in the middle (note the two bead bars);
some kanji scholars view the bottom component as two hands holding the abacus. 筒 (tō, cylinder, as in 水筒 suit , water/cylinder, thermos)
pictures a bamboo object with the same (同) diameter at all points.
Other bamboo-kanji that represent objects produced in pre-cardboard,
pre-plastic ancient China include 箱 (*hako*, 'box') and 箸 (*hashi*, 'chopsticks'). 箸 was added to Japan's official general-use kanji list recently, as was 箋 (*sen*, 'slip of paper', 処方箋 *shoh sen*, 'medical prescription').

Bamboo is useful in the construction of bridges for crossing ravines and rivers.

There is no doubt that humans were using bamboo in all kinds of ways wherever it was found, long before they adopted a written language – and not just in Asia, but throughout the Americas. There is extensive documentation of the multitude of ways in which bamboo has been utilized by human civilizations throughout history, for domestic and culinary use, in architecture, in medicine, and to make musical instruments and weapons, to name just a few applications. It is often said that bamboo is the material of millions from the cradle to the grave. Indeed, in many cultures, a bamboo knife is used to cut the umbilical cord of newborn babies.[6] The umbilical cord is held by the mother's toes and cut by the father with the bamboo knife – which he most likely made himself.[7] A sharp sliver of bamboo is also used in the practice of circumcision in some tribal cultures. And at the end of life in many cultures, burial may take place within a coffin made of woven bamboo, or cremation occurs upon a bamboo pyre. In regions where indigenous people live, bamboo is made into homes, tools and baskets, part of the daily life in such communities. The ethnic group in Mali known as the Bozo takes its name from the Bambara phrase *bo-so*, which means 'bamboo house'. Around the world, buildings old and new, traditional and contemporary, showcase the remarkable versatility of bamboo.

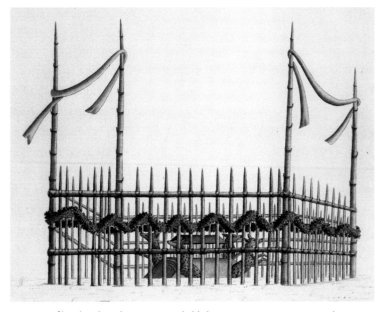

Painting of bamboo burial structure, probably by a European artist, or an Indian artist trained in the European manner, illustrating the burial rituals of tribal groups in the Garo Hills, in Assam, northeastern India.

Traditional bamboo homes on the southwest coast of India.

Over the ages, human ingenuity and modern technologies have innovated more sophisticated applications of bamboo. Examples include water conduits, light-bulb filaments, phonograph needles, aircraft skins, concrete reinforcement, fabric, suspension bridges and charcoal for cooking fuel, as well as water filtration, air purification and engineered plywood.[8]

Even the earliest users of bamboo made the most of its versatility. With it they developed simple tools to hunt and cut meat, and as a material for building shelters and enclosures. The latter could also be used as traps for catching wild animals. The bow and arrow was developed, bamboo being a perfect material for both parts. Later, when humans began to domesticate animals, bamboo enclosures could keep animals penned. Long bamboo poles could reach out into the water to catch fish. Bamboo could be fashioned into ladders and used to reach fruits and other forest products high up in the trees. In addition, new shoots of bamboo, emerging from the ground like asparagus, were found to be a great food source – delectable to eat and quite nutritious.

Bamboo rafts are traditional river craft in many parts of Southeast Asia.

Bamboo baskets are made in all sizes and shapes: they are very affordable, practical and biodegradable.

Watercolour from the early to mid-1800s showing a freshly harvested shoot, a cross-section of the shoot and the source, a bamboo plant, in the background.

The composition of bamboo tissue and the structure of the stem gives the plant unique properties in terms of splitting.[9] With a sharp tool, bamboo can be easily split into thinner, more manageable dimensions, enabling finer manifestations for tasks such as weaving and stitching. In this way woven flat bamboo pieces can be used to make large or small baskets, floor mats, walls and sieves. Bound together to make rope, bamboo can be stretched out lengthwise to create bridges suspended over ravines and rivers. Lashed together, bamboo can become a raft or a boat. Cut pieces of bamboo can be used as fuel – either as they are or burnt into charcoal for a longer-lasting fuel source.[10]

Larger tree-like stems of bamboo can be utilized to construct almost anything wood timbers can be used for; indeed, thanks to

Cut bamboo as raw material awaiting utilization in a timber yard in Ecuador.

bamboo's incredible strength, it goes beyond what traditional woods can do. Sometimes referred to as 'vegetal steel', the inherent strength of bamboo is due to its unique cellular anatomy: the physiology of the arrangement of the interior vascular bundles gives rise to great mechanical properties.[11] For builders, the significant factor is that bamboo's compressive strength is greater than that of concrete and it has the same strength-to-weight ratio as steel in tension. By weight,

Bamboo is the material of choice for construction scaffolding throughout Asia, as here in Gangtok, Sikkim.

bamboo is five times stronger than concrete. It is lighter than steel and grows much faster than trees. Because of its versatility and flexibility, bamboo has long been used as an assembly material throughout regions where it grows naturally. One fascinating application is in the construction of temporary scaffolding. Able to reach as high as any skyscraper, bamboo is strong enough to support the weight of builders, their equipment and materials and, unlike metal scaffolding, bamboo is lightweight and can be tailor-made to suit any type of construction. It is extremely cost-effective, being one-tenth of the price of steel, and can be easily deconstructed and used again on another project. Visit any Asian country today and you will see bamboo scaffolds framing new constructions, traditional material juxtaposed with contemporary architecture. The workers who build and work within this web-like scaffolding are affectionately referred to as 'spiders' because of their gravity-defying skills. For centuries,

overleaf: Intricate tying ensures reliability of support, as shown in this close-up of bamboo scaffolding junctions.

the craft of erecting bamboo scaffolding has been passed down from generation to generation.[12]

Bamboo has other uses, too. Nearly 2,000 years ago, the Chinese discovered firecrackers by accident. Legend has it that while bamboo was being burnt to mark the lunar New Year, it caught fire and air trapped in the hollow stem expanded and burst, resulting in a 'popping' sound. This then was the first firecracker, which provided a very good way indeed to scare away evil spirits. Through experimenting with various combinations, Chinese chemists eventually came up with a mixture that added more volume to the bamboo 'pop'. This explosive mixture was the precursor to today's gunpowder. Ironically, this primitive means of warding off evil has been developed into an integral part of weaponry.[13]

The unique composition of bamboo cell structure has led to other significant applications.[14] The first patented electric lamp comprised a carbonized filament made from bamboo. The noted American inventor Thomas Edison changed the course of modern history with his successful creation of a long-lasting carbon-filament light bulb. In 1879, when he was 32 years old, he succeeded in manufacturing incandescent electric light with a carbonized cotton filament covered with tar and soot, which lasted for 45 hours. Edison believed that the electric light bulb must last for more than 600 hours to be marketable. He obtained more than 6,000 potential filament materials from all over the world to test their effectiveness. One day, he tested a piece of bamboo taken from an oriental fan he found in the laboratory. The filament lasted for 200 hours. Consequently, he began to concentrate his efforts on gathering bamboos from all over the world to test them. He sent more than twenty researchers to many countries in search of the best bamboo for the filament of the electric bulb. It is said to have cost him over $100,000, a good deal of money in the late nineteenth century.

In 1880, one of Edison's researchers, William H. Moore, went to Japan and had the honour of meeting the Japanese prime minister Itō Hirobumi and minister of foreign affairs Yamagata Aritomo. The Japanese statesmen advised Moore to go to Kyoto to obtain the appropriate bamboo. There, Uemura Masanao, the first governor of the Kyoto Prefecture of the new Meiji government, received him and suggested that the bamboos in Sagano and Yawata in Kyoto might be suitable for the filaments of electric bulbs.

The electric bulb with the filament of the *ma-dake* bamboo (*Phyllostachys bambusoides*) from Yawata lasted for 2,450 hours. The Edison General Electric Company was founded to manufacture electric light bulbs with filaments made from the Yawata bamboos, which were exported around the world for about ten years until 1894, when they were replaced by the cellulose filament bulbs. In Japan, Edison is known as 'the King of the Inventions' and there is a monument to him at the top of the sacred Otokoyama Mountain.[15]

Music

Bamboo's natural hollow form makes it an obvious choice for many instruments, particularly wind and percussion. The flute is perhaps the most recognizable bamboo instrument; there are many different kinds of bamboo flute made all over the world, such as the simple Chinese flutes (*dizi* and *xiao*), the *shakuhachi* of Japan and the Philippine *palendag*. Throughout India, the flute is a very popular and highly respected musical instrument; even the poorest person can have one. In India, Nepal and Bangladesh there is a flute called *bansuri*, meaning 'bamboo musical notes' in Sanskrit. The *bansuri* appears everywhere in sculptures and paintings, as Lord Krishna's divine instrument. Four of the instruments used in Polynesia for traditional hula are made of bamboo: the nose flute, rattle, stamping pipes and jaw harp.[16]

Pan flutes, or panpipes, are another group of instruments often made from types of bamboo. Throughout the world both curved and straight assemblages of closed-end bamboo tubes have been employed not only for making music, but also for communication among shepherds and to lure prey.[17]

In China, a *jinghu* (also called the *huqin*) is a type of fiddle, a bowed string instrument. It is popular in Beijing opera, sometimes doubling

The *angklung* is a made of two tubes attached to a bamboo frame. The tubes are carved to have a resonant pitch when struck. The base of the frame is held in one hand, while the other hand strikes the instrument. This causes a repeating note to sound. Each of three or more performers in an *angklung* ensemble plays just one note or more, but altogether complete melodies are produced. The instrument is popular throughout Southeast Asia, but it originated in Indonesia and has been played by the Sudanese for many centuries.

as a singer's voice. Similar bowed fiddles can also be found throughout Southeast Asia, Korea (the *haegum*) and Japan. In performance the musician sits cross-legged, holding the instrument vertically on the left knee. The left hand controls pitch and vibrato by pulling the strings towards the neck; there is no fingerboard. With the right hand the performer moves the bow horizontally between the strings while controlling the tension of the horsehair. The sound is quite distinct and can be extremely high-pitched.[18]

In Indonesia and the Philippines, bamboo has long been used for making various kinds of musical instrument including the *kolintang*, *angklung* and *bumbong*. Traditional Philippine *banda kawayan* (bamboo bands) use a variety of traditional bamboo musical instruments, as well as remarkable bamboo versions of Western instruments such as clarinets, saxophones and tubas.[19]

Mouth organs are another creative musical instrument traditionally constructed using bamboo. The *sheng* of China and the *khen* of Lao origin are both mouth organs whose pipes, made of bamboo, are connected with a small, hollowed-out hardwood or gourd reservoir into which air is blown, creating a sound similar to that of the violin. On the Indian Ocean side of Africa, the island of Madagascar has the *valiha*, a long tube zither made of a single bamboo stalk, which is considered the national instrument.[20]

The jaw (Jew's or mouth) harp is one of the oldest musical instruments in the world. Its origins are in ancient China, where paintings of people playing a small bamboo musical instrument date back as far as the third century BC. Over the following centuries, the jaw harp quickly spread throughout Asia and the Middle East. By the thirteenth century AD, the jaw harp was found in all parts of Europe. During this time, it became popular in just about every culture from East Asia to Western Europe, and is known now by over 800 different names in many parts of the world. Jaw harps were constructed of bamboo, wood, bone or a metal such as brass during these early centuries, but today the instrument is almost exclusively constructed of modern metals.[21]

Bamboo may be used in the construction of all kinds of instrument: traditional, contemporary or otherwise. The Australian didgeridoo, for example, as well as all sorts of percussion instruments, can be made from bamboo, not just the more traditional eucalyptus. The Yamaha Corporation of America pioneered new manufacturing processes incorporating bamboo's sonic and ecological benefits into traditional Western instruments, and is now using the material to make guitars and drums more sustainably. Conventional guitars and drums are usually made from slow-growing hardwoods like cedar, rosewood and mahogany, which are difficult to replenish. Bamboo shares many of the same desirable properties with these woods, but matures quickly and can be grown on a rotating basis for continual replenishment. By varying the orientation of bamboo's long, straight fibres, Yamaha makes the most of the material's natural strength and warp resistance. The result is a sound that is remarkably bright and clear.[22]

A unique example of the sound of bamboo can be heard in the music of the band TakéDaké, led by John Kaizan Neptune. TakéDaké literally means 'Bamboo Only' in Japanese. All of the instruments used are made by band members out of bamboo.

And where there is music, there is song. Bamboo is referenced in many ways in many songs, which refer to its traditional symbolic aspects (strength, flexibility and versatility) as well as telling humorous anecdotes. In the British musical film *Chitty Chitty Bang Bang* (1968). Caractacus Potts, played by Dick Van Dyke, takes part in a light-spirited song and dance number entitled 'Me Ol' Bamboo', the subject of which is men and their various usages of cane-like 'tools'. Songwriter Robert B. Sherman was inspired to write the song by his own use of a bamboo walking stick, which he used after a knee injury sustained during the Second World War. Another celebration of bamboo in song is 'The Big Bamboo', an often-covered Calypso number written by Slinger Francisco in the 1950s. It plays fun at the comparison of the bamboo shoot to the male penis, and is narrated by a man asking his woman how he can make her happy and keep her true. Her reply is that the only thing she wants is a piece of 'that big bamboo'. Other verses compare the size of bamboo to other plants, such as sugar cane and banana, but her reply is always that she only wants the big bamboo, which 'pleases one and all'.

Contemporary bamboo guitar from China, completed with American artistic expression by Wes Baldwin of North Carolina, USA.

Bamboo in Games and Sport

It is not surprising to find games and sport around the world involving bamboo. Children have often found ways of entertaining themselves with bamboo, whether by using a simple cut pole as a toy sword or as a baseball bat, and many of these games have caught on, evolved and spread. And not just games for children – many adult entertainments incorporate bamboo in some way, such as Kau Cim and table games such as Mahjong.

Kau Cim is a fortune-telling practice originating in China, also known as Chien Tung or Chinese Fortune Sticks. The *cim* refers to a bucket, traditionally a bamboo cup or tube, which contains sticks generally made from bamboo as well, often painted red at one end. A single number, both in Arabic numerals and in Chinese characters, is marked on each stick – this denotes the fortune, which is outlined in an accompanying reference book. In the U.S., a version has been sold since 1915 under the name Chi Chi Sticks. Kau Cim is also sometimes known as 'The Oracle of Kuan Yin' in Buddhist traditions.[23]

Mahjong is a game played on a table consisting of tiles – originally made from bone or bamboo, or often bone backed with bamboo. Today, most modern sets are constructed from various plastics such as bakelite, celluloid and more recently nylon. In addition, aside from the actual tiles being originally made of bamboo, one of the three categories (suits) is the bamboo suit.[24] One of the myths about the origin of Mahjong claims that Confucius, the Chinese philosopher, developed the game in about 500 BC; whatever its origin, Mahjong is a game of skill, strategy and calculation, and involves a riveting degree of chance.

Moving off the table and into the playground, we might encounter *chinlone*, a type of football played extensively in Myanmar. It is related to similar games in Southeast Asia known as *takraw* in Thailand, *sepak raga* in Malaysia, Singapore and Indonesia, *sipa* in the Philippines, *kator* in Laos and *da cau* in Vietnam. *Sepak takraw*, a competitive variation of the game played over a net, was developed in Malaysia in the 1940s.

Photograph of the competition at the Kendo European Championships in Bern, Switzerland, in 2005, by Harald Hofer. The kendo sword is made of bamboo.

The origins of *chinlone* may be associated with the ancient Chinese game of *cuju* or *tsu chu*, which is acknowledged by Fédération Internationale de Football Association (FIFA) as being the oldest form of soccer. A similar game is also played in Japan, where it is known as *kemari*. *Chinlone* is related to the family of sports played by kicking a shuttlecock, known as *jianzi* in China and Taiwan, and *jegichagi* in Korea. There is some evidence to suggest that a version of such games travelled across the Bering Strait and influenced Native Americans, who also played a variety of games involving keeping a ball up with the feet. These games are thought to be the origin of footbag, also known as hacky sack, seen today in many parks and on university campuses.[25]

Chinlone is a game of skill and dexterity. The 'ball' is made of bamboo or rattan.

However, nowhere in the world has the level of extraordinary foot skills and dexterity been combined with artistic expression and spirituality as in the Myanmar game of *chinlone*. It is a combination of sport and dance, a team sport with no opposing team. On no account must the ball hit the ground. In essence *chinlone* is non-competitive, yet it is as demanding as the most competitive ball game. The focus is not on winning or losing, but on how beautifully one plays the game.

Chinlone dates back at least to the Pyu era (seventh century). According to U Ye Aung, Deputy Secretary of the Myanmar Chinlone Federation, 'There was a pagoda near Kalakan Kone village, Hmyaw Sar town in Pyi district; when the pagoda collapsed and archaeological excavations were carried out to examine the objects that were buried in the ground, they found a silver cane ball under the remains of pagoda.' In the past, *chinlone* balls were woven from strips of palm leaf or bamboo although cane (rattan) is now used. Traditionally,

opposite: The tiles used in the Chinese tile game of Mahjong were originally made of bamboo, or of a combination of bone and bamboo. Additionally, one of the 'suits' of Mahjong is bamboo.

chinlone was played at pagoda festivals and at monks' funerals. Ever growing in popularity, *chinlone* is now played not only as part of entertainment programmes, but as a leisure activity.[26]

There are many games played throughout the Philippines which involve bamboo. One, *bati-cobra*, is played outdoors as a hitting and catching game between two or more players. To play this game, two bamboo sticks (one long and one short) are used. One player acts as batter and stands opposite the others at a distance. The shorter stick is used as a ball would be in baseball, the longer stick being the bat, so the player tosses the shorter stick and strikes it with the longer one. The other players then attempt to catch the flying shorter stick. Whoever catches the stick goes up to bat next. If no one succeeds in catching it, any player can then pick it up. At this point the batter will put down the longer stick, and the holder of the shorter stick will throw it in an attempt to hit the longer stick on the ground. If the longer stick is hit, the player who threw the shorter stick becomes the next batter; if the player who threw the shorter stick misses, the same batter will continue.[27]

Another amusing game played throughout the Philippines is *palo-sebo*: greased bamboo pole climbing! The game is more of an attraction than a sport, as obviously the spectators enjoy it as much as the players. It is usually played during town fiestas. The objective of the players is to be the first to reach the prize, a small bag (usually containing money or toys) located at the top of the bamboo pole.[28]

Pole vaulting is another sport in which the bamboo pole had a role to play. Pole vaults were originally sharpened bamboo sticks which were jabbed into the ground for leverage. When the sport started to be taken more seriously, the bamboo pole was replaced with tubular steel, fibreglass and carbon composites.

Fishing (whether as a means of hunting or as a sport) makes perfect use of the bamboo pole. Long and tapering, with a simple loop at one end and a line of string held in the hand, lightweight bamboo poles aided early fishermen by extending out over the water. The natural

opposite: Traditional uses of bamboo as both raft and fishing pole, Southeast Asia.

Beyond the simple fishing pole, modern-day bamboo fly-fishing rods are highly prized works of art as well as being exceptionally good for catching fish.

characteristics of the tapering pole and the segmented stem allowed further refinements – poles could be engineered into separate pieces so that they could be conveniently dismantled for transportation and storage, and easily reassembled along the waterway. Today, the finest fly-fishing rods in the world are made from bamboo.[29]

Increasingly, modern games and sports are integrating bamboo, as recent technologies in engineered bamboo products have led to bamboo becoming an alternative to traditional hardwoods. Baseball bats, skateboards, surfboards and even bicycles are being modelled out of bamboo. Hape International is a brand of children's toys with a social conscience which hosted an international UNESCO workshop in Anji, China, in 2004. Focusing on bamboo as an environmentally friendly and sustainable material, and specializing in well-designed toys, Hape became the first toy company to design, produce and globally distribute a wide range of toys made of bamboo.

Folktales, Allegories and Literature

In addition to its practical uses, bamboo has been woven into folklore and legends, as well as into art, music and literature. The tall, straight and beautiful bamboo has been a favourite image of Chinese scholars and artists, who have sung its praises since ancient times. References to bamboo can be found in the creation beliefs of cultures spread across the globe (India, Japan, China, Indonesia and Colombia), while the mythologies of several early cultures regard the empty bamboo culm (the hollow stem) as the womb of the race.

According to mythology of the Patangoros tribe of Colombia, there was a great flood which resulted in only one man surviving. For many years he wandered in loneliness and sorrow, but one day the Heaven Master (or God) took pity on him and came down to Earth, bringing with him two pieces of bamboo. He transformed one piece into a woman, to provide the lonely man with a companion, and with the other piece he built them a house.[30]

Taro and the Bamboo Shoot is a wonderful Japanese tale of a boy who goes out to cut a bamboo shoot and instead hitches a ride to the sky as the shoot elongates. The story was written by Masako Matsuno and illustrated by Yasuo Segawa in 1964.

On the other side of the world, the Piyumi tribe in Taiwan believed that the first man and woman of their ancestors came from different internodes of the same culm of a bamboo plant. Since then, bamboo has given them shelter and protection.[31]

According to Philippine folk tales, the creation story told in the ethnic language of tagalog (now standardized as modern Filipino) runs as follows:

When the world first began there was no land, but only the sea and the sky, and between them was a kite. One day the bird, which had nowhere to land, grew tired of flying about, so she stirred up the sea until it threw its waters against the sky. The sky, in order to restrain the sea, showered upon it many islands until it could no longer rise, but ran back and forth. Then the sky ordered the kite to light on one of the islands to build her nest, and to leave the sea and the sky in peace.

Now at this time the land breeze and the sea breeze were married, and they had a child which was a bamboo. One day when this bamboo was floating about on the water, it bumped into the feet of the kite which was on the beach. The bird, angry that anything should strike it, pecked at the bamboo, and out of one section came a man and from the other a woman.

Then the earthquake called on all the birds and fish to see what should be done with these two, and it was decided that they should marry. Many children were born to the couple, and from them came all the different races of people.[32]

A somewhat different account of the origin of man is given by the Marindineeze, a tribe that occupies the flats on the southern coast of West Papua, Indonesia:

They say that one day a crane was busy picking fish out of the sea. He threw them onto the beach, where the clay washed over, covering and killing them. So the fish were no longer anything but shapeless lumps of clay. It is said that the lumps of clay were cold and so they warmed themselves at a fire made of bamboos. Every time that a little bamboo burst with a pop in the heat, the lumps of clay assumed more and more the shape of human beings. Thus the apertures of their ears, eyes, mouth and nostrils were opened, but as yet they could not speak, they could only utter a murmuring sound. Their fingers were still joined by membranes like those in the wings of bats. However, with a bamboo knife they severed the membranes and threw them into the sea, where they turned into leeches. When the nature spirit (a mythical ancestral being) saw the human beings, he was very upset, and enviously questioned the crane, why he had bestowed life on these creatures. So the crane ceased to peck at the fish and pecked at a log of wood instead; and that is why his beak has been bent ever since. At last, while the first men were sitting around the fire, a big bamboo burst with a louder crack than usual, which terribly frightened the people so that they gave a loud shriek, and that was the beginning of human speech.[33]

Many other Asian cultures, including that of the Andaman Islands, also believe that all of humanity emerged from a bamboo stem. Malaysian legends tell a similar story of a man who dreams of a beautiful woman while sleeping under a bamboo plant; he wakes up and breaks the bamboo stem, discovering the woman inside. Hawaiian bamboo (*'Ohe*) is just one of the forms taken by the Polynesian creator god, Kāne. However, probably the most popular creation story involving bamboo is *The Tale of the Bamboo Cutter* (竹取物語, *Taketori Monogatari*). This Japanese folktale from the tenth century, considered one of the oldest surviving Japanese narratives, details the life of a mysterious girl who was discovered as a baby inside the stem of a bamboo plant. There are several variations on this theme, with titles such as *The Tale of the Shining Princess*, *The Moon*

Princess and *The Bamboo Princess*. In *Takenoko Doji*, a carpenter's apprentice is cutting bamboo in a bamboo grove, when he hears a voice asking to be 'let out'. The apprentice cuts the bamboo, and a 5-inch man emerges. He says he is called Takenoko Doji and that he is 1,234 years old, and offers to grant the apprentice seven wishes. The apprentice wishes to become a samurai. In another tale called *Takehime*, a beautiful girl comes out of a piece of bamboo cut by a poor man. When she is ten years old, she returns to heaven, leaving behind her a red container for rice and a ladle.[34]

Another wonderful allegory is the ancient Vietnamese legend *The Hundred-knot Bamboo Tree*, which tells of a poor, young farmer who falls in love with his landlord's beautiful daughter. The farmer asks the landlord for his daughter's hand in marriage, but the proud landlord will not allow her to be bound in marriage to a poor farmer. The landlord decides to foil the marriage with an impossible deal: the farmer must bring him a 'bamboo tree of one hundred nodes'. But Buddha appears to the farmer and tells him that such a tree can be made from one hundred nodes using several different bamboo culms. Buddha gives him four magic words to attach together the many nodes of bamboo: 'Khắc nhập, khắc xuất', which means 'joined together immediately, fall apart immediately'. The triumphant farmer returns to the landlord and demands his daughter. Curious to see such a long bamboo, the landlord is magically joined to the bamboo when he touches it as the young farmer says the first two magic words. The story ends with the happy marriage of the farmer and the landlord's daughter once the landlord agrees to the marriage and asks to be separated from the bamboo.[35]

The symbolism throughout folktales and literature acknowledges bamboo in many ways. In China and Japan, the word 'bamboo' alludes to abundant life, bearing adversity, fastidiousness, fidelity, gentleness, gracefulness, long life, modesty, open-mindedness, peace, refinement, straightforwardness, tranquillity, righteousness, winter, yielding but enduring strength and protection against defilement. Other words combined with bamboo have additional meanings: in Japan the bam-

Japanese hanging scroll of the Seven Sages of the Bamboo Grove
painted by Tsutsumi Torin III (1743–1820).

boo and the crane together symbolize longevity and happiness, while
the bamboo grove symbolizes the everyday world, and a family of
princes. In China and India, the bamboo and tiger together signify
safety. In India, bamboo is a symbol of friendship, while in Southeast
Asia, it is referred to as 'brother'. It stands for constancy because it
remains evergreen throughout the year; fidelity because of its resili-
ence in winter snows; integrity because when broken and split, its parts
remain straight and even; purity because its heart is always empty
and clean; rectitude because it bends without breaking under stress
and stands up straight again.[36]

Along with the pine and the plum, the bamboo is also part of
the plant trinity representing Lao Tzu, who was born beneath a plum
tree; the Buddha, who died in a bamboo grove; and Confucius – the
Three Friends of the cold season. This trio suggests that those who
encounter hardship should never falter, for these three flourish despite
adverse conditions.[37]

This trio, the Three Friends of Winter, is known as 'Sho-Chiku-Bai' in Japanese. *Sho* means pine, *chiku* bamboo and *bai* plum. This combination is considered auspicious. Pine and bamboo are evergreen; pine is associated with longevity, and bamboo with strength coupled with flexibility; plum trees are the first to bloom each year, sometimes when there is still snow on the ground. In Japan, green bamboo symbolizes purity.[38]

In China, the bamboo is one of the Four Noble Plants, along with the plum blossom, the orchid and the chrysanthemum. These plants also exhibit characteristics alluding to virtuous traits in a gentleman, and are referenced throughout ancient and modern Chinese literature. In traditional Chinese culture, bamboo is a metaphor of vitality and longevity, which usually relates to a man of exemplary conduct and nobility of character. Silently grown in desolate mountains, bamboo is very slim (compared to tree trunks) with joints on its stem and leaves like sheaths. As a reward for faithfulness, bamboos reaching for the sky are transformed into rainbows symbolizing true love. The plant was also thought to produce no flowers in the spring in order not to compete with others, while its rapid growth was a model of ambition.[39]

The firm and indomitable willpower of bamboo was admired by many ancient writers and painters. Su Dongpo, the famous Chinese poet of the Song Dynasty (960–1279), wrote, 'I would rather eat without meat than live without bamboo.' Zheng Banqiao, a celebrated Qing Dynasty painter and calligrapher, devoted his whole life to painting bamboo. It became a mark of the expressionistic Southern School (literati painting) in China. The student learns that bamboos are never the same, and the artist is counselled to observe every turning leaf in the wind, every droop laden by moisture, and each leaf bent under by snow.[40]

The first mention of bamboo in ancient writings was by Ctesias, a Greek historian on Persia and India (and the court physician of King Artaxerxes Mnemom of Persia), in 400 BC:

opposite: Grown in the countryside and in the garden, bamboo is a symbol that celebrates daily life, as here in Vietnam.

A glazed porcelain jar of the Chongzhen period of the Ming Dynasty, China. *c.* 1643.

The river Indus flows across plains and between mountains, where the Indian reed [bamboo] grows. It is so thick that two men can hardly get their arms round it, and as tall as the mast of a merchant-ship of largest tonnage. Some are larger, some smaller, as is natural considering the size of the mountain.[41]

The first mention of bamboo in Western writings deals with a physical description of what has been determined to be bamboo plants growing in the wild. It appeared, as mentioned previously, in a letter from Alexander the Great to Aristotle, and is referred to by Pliny (AD 23–79) in his *Natural History*:

Woodblock print made in 1788 by Kitagawa Utamaro from a collection of *kyōka* (literally 'crazy verse'). Poetry circles sprang up for competition and recreation, and often commissioned illustrated anthologies and single-sheet prints of their finest work. Each page in the book features two poems about two different insects, along with illustrations of both insects and plants. The two poems on this page are about a mole cricket and an earwig. Utamaro illustrated the insects using a bamboo shoot.

Seki-sai, bamboo sketch painted on paper, Japan, 1800–80.

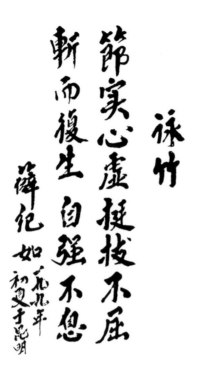

Xue Jiru penned this poem, 'Song in Praise of Bamboo', in 1998, expressing respect for bamboo and as a metaphor for the human condition.

internode hard
centre empty
yet upright
without bending

after cutting
the bamboo character
finds no death
rebirth
sprouting from
defeat
without
bending

In every variety of the reed [bamboo] a single root gives birth to numerous stems, and if cut down, they will shoot again with increased fecundity. The root, which is naturally tenacious of life, is also jointed as well as the stem. The reeds of India are the only ones in which the leaves are short; but in all the varieties these leaves take their rise at the joints, and surround the stem with a fine tissue about half way upwards to the next joint, and then leave the stem and droop downwards. The reed, as well as the calamus, although rounded, has two sides, which throw out leaves alternately from above the joints, in such a way that when one springs from the right side, the next issues from the joint above it on the left, and so in turns. Branches, too, shoot occasionally from the stem, being themselves reeds of diminutive growth.[42]

98

Medicine

Bamboo has been used in native pharmacopoeia since ancient times, among many early tribal groups in the Americas, as well as throughout India and Asia. Derivatives of bamboo are still used in Chinese and Indian medicines, and among tribal groups around the world for various local remedies and cures. Numerous medical virtues are ascribed to all parts of the plant: the roots, shoots, internodes, leaves, flowers, fruits and the water that accumulates in the interior of the culm. Oil extracted from the stems, sap from the internodes, rhizomes, roots, leaves and mineral accumulations are used for a variety of specialized cures, aphrodisiacs, nutritional supplements, remedies and more.

In Ayurveda, the Indian system of traditional medicine, the siliceous precipitate found in the culms of the bamboo stem is called *banslochan*.[43] It is also known as *tabashir* (*tabasheer* or *tawashir* in Unani-tibb, the Indo-Persian system of medicine). In English it is also called 'bamboo manna'. This is a loose, solid deposit existing within the culm-internode that is detected by a rattling sound when shaking the culm. It consists of almost pure salicylic acid (essentially aspirin as it is known in the Western world) and is found within many bamboo species. *Tabashir* may be chalky or transparent, of white or bluish-white colour. In most Indian literature, *Bambusa arundinacea* (syn. *bambos*) is described as the source of bamboo manna, as well as *B. vulgaris*, *Dendrocalamus asper* and *Melocanna baccifera*. In traditional medicine, it is thought to reduce fever and eliminate phlegm. It is used as a cooling tonic, to draw poison out of wounds and as an aphrodisiac.[44]

The raw shoot sap of *Bambusa vulgaris* is used to treat fever, coughs and phlegm congestion, while chopped leaves have been analysed to reveal anti-carcinoma properties and bioantioxidant activity.[45] In a publication from China in 1707, it was said that eating bamboo shoots cures ulcers, while in Tibetan pharmacology, medicines containing bamboo manna are used to treat inflammations of the lungs.[46] Fermented succulent shoots of *Dendrocalamus giganteus* have been shown to be an enriched source of phytosterols, leading to the production of steroidal drugs.[47]

Almost anyone who frequents a Chinese restaurant knows that bamboo shoots are edible. Pickled, dried, frozen or fresh bamboo shoots are a low-calorie source of potassium and protein. The protein found within bamboo shoots contains at least seventeen kinds of amino acid and carbohydrate that can be absorbed by the human body.[48]

In addition, bamboo shoots contain magnesium and an element called germanium, both of which are said to have anti-cancer and anti-ageing functions, as well as zinc, manganese, chromium and other trace elements.[49] All of this makes bamboo shoots nutritious to eat, as well as a useful source of medicinal products.

A delicious bamboo shoot salad, compliments of Daphne Lewis (www.bamboofarmingusa.com).

Delicious and nutritious, grilled bamboo shoots can be enjoyed in many recipes.

four

Modern Potentials, Today and Tomorrow

The global market for bamboo is currently estimated at U.S.$7 billion per year. This amount is expected to grow to nearly $17 billion a year by 2017.[1] While the traditional bamboo market has been driven primarily by small handicrafts and household goods, future uses of bamboo are likely to include commercial applications such as building materials and flooring, bio-based composites, fibre and pulp, transportation, alternative energies, pharmacology and environmental remedies such as erosion control and using bamboo in phyto-remediation projects. Trading in bamboo, from raw materials to value-added products, from shoots to furniture, from charcoal to flooring, has the potential to make a great contribution to the global market as an environmentally sustainable product.[2]

Bamboo as Timber Substitute

As previously mentioned, bamboo is stronger than wood in tension and compression. The tensile strength of the fibres of a vascular bundle can be up to 12,000 kilograms per square centimetre – almost twice that of steel.[3] Late twentieth-century scientific research and engineering brought bamboo into modern consideration,[4] and better understanding of the anatomy of the bamboo culm and research into its material properties and techniques for preservation has led to improved efficiency in its use.[5] Interest in bamboo as a viable material came with the awareness that bamboo is the fastest growing plant on Earth

Bamboo charcoal is used primarily as fuel for home cooking, drying tea and water purification, as well as to eliminate organic impurities and unpleasant smells.

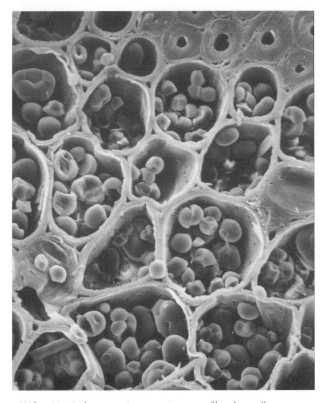

Walter Liese's electron-microscope imagery of bamboo cell structure.

One method of preserving bamboo involves pushing the sap out of the bamboo stems (Boucherie system) to prevent degradation.

Esterílla is the term used for the lumber made from breaking open and flattening a bamboo culm. After it has been flattened it can be used for walls, floors and anywhere else a flat piece of lumber is needed.

and its wide distribution makes it a valuable natural resource in view of diminishing tropical forests and the inadequate supply of timber from natural forests.

Flattened bamboo culms, referred to as *esteríllas* or *bahareques* in South America, have been used for hundreds of years in some communities to create walls, roofs and floors. With the advent of modern bamboo technologies this practice is now becoming widespread, and bamboo flooring, plywood and panels are common.[6] Bamboo (whole or split) can also be used to create a sturdy reinforcing framework within a construction, a building method known as *quincha* in Peru.[7] These methods will no doubt continue to be used and improved upon. Investigations into combining materials are being undertaken, such as using re-formed bamboo, glass fabric and aluminium together. Such combinations are referred to as 'super-hybrid' eco-materials.[8] This hybridization can be effective in increasing the compressive tensile strength of the composite material. The recyclability of reformed bamboo ensures that this material is environmentally friendly, and as such its use could help save natural forest resources.

Today, bamboo building products are widely available in the global market. They include laminated bamboo boards, mainly used in flooring and cabinetry applications, for example the brand Plyboo®, and engineered dimensional lumber such as Lumboo®.[9] Bamboo fibreboards, mat boards and veneers can also be found; for exterior applications, bamboo composites can be used for decking. This consists of a type of composite material made by mixing natural bamboo fibre with 100 per cent recycled plastics. This construction-grade material is a strong, moisture-resistant composite engineered to withstand rain, rot, snow, ice, sand and road pollution. The surface has the appearance of natural wood and requires minimal maintenance. Products such as these answer the call for environmentally friendly alternatives to traditional wood and plastic decking and are marketed accordingly.

The recent trend in 'branding' bamboo as a green material is based on the belief that bamboo represents a sustainable, cost-effective and

A modern-day bridge built of bamboo in the Netherlands, designed by
Pim de Blaey and Charley Younge.

ecologically benign alternative to the widespread clearcutting of
old-growth forests and dwindling timber resources. Because bamboo
grows back after cutting, it is a renewable resource. Much like a giant
lung, a living forest breathes. It has been estimated that bamboo's leafy
canopy releases 35 per cent more oxygen than a comparable cluster of
hardwood trees, especially since the bamboo regrows and reproduces
a canopy many times in its lifespan.[10] During the renewing process,
the bamboo plant grabs carbon dioxide from the air and holds it
within its culm and root system, not releasing it until the soil in which
the plant decomposes is cultivated. It is becoming generally accepted
that one major cause of climate change is the rising levels of gases in the
Earth's atmosphere, the most dangerous being carbon dioxide. Products
made from bamboo take that carbon out of circulation. Bamboo products which are sustainably harvested and properly manufactured can last
for many generations, keeping carbon locked up throughout the life
of the products and helping to offset carbon usage that occurs during
manufacture and shipping.[11]

opposite: House construction primarily of bamboo is common in regions
where bamboo is the local natural resource and is readily available.

Contemporary bamboo roof architecture – elegance and style.

Modern electronic products on display at the Consumer Electronics Show, Las Vegas. .

opposite: As bamboo stems age or after they are cut,
they lose their green colour and turn beige.

Contemporary, simple, functional and biodegradable bamboo bowls from Southeast Asia.

Bamboo Architecture

Colombian engineering pioneer Oscar Hidalgo-Lopez spent his lifetime investigating the possibilities of using the abundant natural resource of his country, the bamboo *Guadua*. In the 1960s, the giant bamboos of Colombia were on the brink of extinction due to the intensive destruction of natural bamboo forests. Thanks to the efforts of the Colombian Institute of Natural Resources, laws were passed to forbid the cutting of bamboo without permission, and since then the bamboo forests and Colombia's forestry industry have thrived.[12]

Hidalgo was followed by Colombian architect Simón Vélez, German bridge-builder Joerg Stamm and countless young carpenters, builders, craftsmen and architects, all of whom were convinced of bamboo's potential as a timber substitute. Recent progress in preservation, construction technologies, joinery improvements, footing techniques and prefabrication have led to impressive discoveries and inspiring structures. Demonstrating the incredible durability and versatility of bamboo, architects are doing more than creating new trends in building; they are promoting the benefits of sustainable living.

It was not that the 'old ways' of building with bamboo were wrong; in fact, lessons learned from researching traditional construction methods in Africa, Peru, Ecuador, Japan, India, Indonesia and beyond have led to a blending of old and new design techniques that not only look fabulous, but make sense. In earthquake-prone areas such as Armenia in Colombia, which suffered a catastrophic quake in 1999, traditional homes built using bamboo have proved better able to withstand the tremors than those made of concrete.[13] As in the bamboo grove, the bamboo can sway, rather than break. The earthquake resistance of bamboo buildings is the result of the strength, lightness and flexibility of the material, which lessens the inertial mass that the walls must support.

Textiles and Fibre

Recent technologies have developed a method of processing bamboo cellulose to allow it to be spun into viscose yarn, like the system

Bamboo houses in India.

High style with modern materials. Bamboo veneer ceiling in Madrid's Barajas airport.

of pulping bamboo to make paper. The process has been criticized as environmentally unfriendly due to the chemicals used; however, there are research and engineering developments underway investigating 'greener' processing, which would utilize natural enzymes rather than caustic chemicals.[14] Any clothing traditionally made of cotton can be made of bamboo fibre, from socks and shirts to bed sheets and bath towels.

In other areas of industrial material innovation, there have been advancements in renewable options to reinforce composites, for example using bamboo fibres in materials like fibreglass, thermoplastics and plastic-moulded composites.[15] Not only are these products 'greener', they are attractive, and bamboo fibre matting is now manufactured as reinforced epoxy resin that can be used as 'skin' in automobile and

Bamboo motif wallpaper design using both English and Japanese influences, made in 1872 by Edward William Godwin in the UK for a booming wallpaper industry.

Bathroom tissue from U.S. company BumBoosa is made with 100% bamboo, sourced from a FSC-certified supplier in China.

aeronautic manufacturing, as well as on products such as surfboards and skateboards.

Bamboo bioplastics have a future, replacing polyplastics that contain Bisphenol A (BPA), a substance under investigation by the United States Food and Drug Administration (FDA) and of concern to government agencies around the world.[16] BPA is an industrial chemical used to make polycarbonate plastic, and is a suspected carcinogen. Bioplastics are used in the manufacture of a wide variety of home and food-service items that involve direct contact with food and drink, such as water bottles, baby bottles, plates and cups, and containers for food storage and microwaving .

Bioplastics are made with plant fibres and vegetable resins, so they are completely compostable and biodegradable, breaking down in landfills and garden compost bins. Bamboo bioplastic is a very promising alternative to existing bioplastics because of the negative

Contemporary uses such as biodegradable disposable products help reduce reliance on paper products derived from timber sources and petroleum-based plastics.

impact of the latter on oil prices, the environment and human health.[17] Its potential uses are endless – as a replacement for all sorts of polyplastic containers, utensils, floor coverings, refuse disposal bags, polystyrene and packaging materials, as well as automobile parts, pipes, insulation and much more.[18]

Transportation

In our early history, when man reached for the sky, it was with the help of bamboo. From kite-flying to hang-gliding and ultra-light aircraft, bamboo had a role to play. Aviation pioneers made use of whole or split bamboo poles since the material was both strong and lightweight. In the mid-1990s, Michel Abadie, now president of the World Bamboo Organization, selected bamboo as the material in the design of a model aircraft.[19] The project, Flyboo, which created a series of ultra-light aircraft models entirely of bamboo, aims to promote innovative contemporary uses of bamboo and position it as a promising material for the future – strong, light and renewable. The bamboo planes also act as a reminder of bamboo's role in enabling humans to fly – symbolizing its ultimate potential.

Designer and innovator Michel Abadie sits on his Flyboo ultra-light aircraft in Paris.

Bamboo can also be found in nautical contexts. Asian boat building evolved from the simple bamboo sailing raft of ancient times, which is still in use in many parts of the world. Indeed, the design of the modern sailing ship is essentially derived from the structure of bamboo – a hollow form strengthened by cross-sectional supports. Bamboo battens and booms are common in contemporary sailing vessels, and entire boats can be made out of bamboo composite materials. In 2010, an 82-foot schooner, *Coracle*, was built by Dirk Schelling as a fine example of a modern-day bamboo sailing vessel.

Another innovative modern use of bamboo is in bicycle frames. These are traditionally made from welded metal tubes, lightweight steel and, more recently, carbon. The first bamboo bike was in fact built in England in 1894, but recently bamboo has become the 'new' material for bicycles.[20] Bicycle frames require great strength and flexibility, to bear the burden of the rider and the unevenness of the road surface. The unique cellular structure of a bamboo stem gives the plant strength comparable to traditional bicycle frame materials, and at the same stiffness bamboo is a similar weight to steel, though considerably heavier than carbon. Bicycle designer and builder Craig Calfee maintains that the best thing bamboo brings to the bicycle is vibration damping, making for a smooth, comfortable ride.[21]

Drawing of an Indian river scene of a boat with bamboo awning by British artist George Chinnery (1775–1857).

Along with the artisan appeal of bamboo bikes, the availability of the material makes their manufacture an ideal cottage industry for the developing world. Calfee joined with Columbia University's Earth Institute to develop a project called Bamboosero, based in Ghana and Uganda.[22] The project trains local people in design and mechanics,

'Aluboo' (bamboo alloy) bicycle frame made by James Wolf of Boo Bicycles.

providing the population with much-needed employment and transportation. Bamboosero has been a huge success, and bamboo bicycle workshops and manufacturing facilities are now to be found throughout other countries in Africa and further afield.

Bamboo as an Energy Source

Bamboo can produce energy via gasification, along with a range of valuable by-products. It can utilize waste generated by existing processing operations, be a substitute for fossil fuels and lower the operating costs of industrial manufacturing.[23] Bamboo was successfully used in the distillation of a diesel-type fuel oil in 1947, and as a raw material for the production of ethanol in 1981.[24]

In the cultivation, harvesting and production of bamboo for various products, there are waste by-products, just as in any other agro-processing endeavour. However, bamboo 'waste' is an excellent source material for alternative fuel products, such as high-grade charcoal and activated carbon.[25] Bamboo-activated carbon is antibacterial, anti-fungal and absorbs odours.[26] It also adsorbs harmful pollutants in the air and water, regulates humidity, and absorbs and emits far-infrared radiation. It releases beneficial negative ions.[27] It is used in gas purification, metal extraction, water purification, medicine, sewage treatment, air filters in gas masks and respirators, compressed air filters and much else. Carbon adsorption has numerous environmental applications in removing pollutants from air or water both in the field and in industrial processes, such as clean-ups of spills, groundwater remediation, drinking-water filtration, air purification, and capturing volatile organic compounds from paints, gasoline and other toxic processes. Activated charcoal is also used in the measurement of radon gas.

In agricultural and forestry applications, charcoal is used as a soil enhancer, promoting healthy root systems and enhancing soil micronutrients which support plant growth. This 2,000-year-old practice converts agricultural waste (the burning of biomass) into a charcoal that holds carbon and improves soil functions, yielding more productivity. Bamboo charcoal can absorb excessive moisture in the soil and when the soil dries out, the trapped moisture gets released back into the soil. It has ten times more surface area than regular charcoal and an absorption rate four times greater.[28]

In other parts of the world, bamboo charcoal production is being used to promote sustainable economic development where firewood consumption is a major cause of deforestation and air pollution.[29] Because bamboo has advantages like self-regeneration, sustainability of supply and environmental benefits, and bamboo charcoal has high heating value, it is very suitable as a household energy source.

Pharmacology

An important by-product of charcoal production is vinegar. Bamboo vinegar is not ingested orally; it is inedible and not a food supplement. Used externally, it has been found to soften skin, repel insects, relieve itching, reduce foot odour, relieve athlete's food, improve blood circulation, eliminate inflammation and help the body to expel unnecessary waste (detoxification).[30] Additionally, the use of bamboo in the cosmetic industry is gaining acceptance. Extracts of bamboo contain high concentrations of naturally occurring silica, which is known to have restorative effects on the skin. It is extracted from bamboo leaves and stems of several species of bamboo, and found in cosmetic products in the form of silica gels, soaps, exfoliants and topical lotions.[31] There is a growing public preference for natural ingredients over the manufactured chemical components found in cosmetics, so it is likely that we will see an increase in bamboo extracts being used in hair and body-care products.

Bamboo also has pharmaceutical potential. Beneficial compounds can be extracted from bamboo leaves (phytochemical leaf extracts); these consist of flavone-rich phenolic compounds that have high-antioxidant qualities, known to be beneficial to human health. These compounds could be utilized as a food additive or supplement, as

Freshly dug bamboo shoots, straight from the bamboo grove.

they may possess co-enzymes with the ability to inhibit cancer-cell pro-duction.[32] So its use in traditional medicine certainly has some basis.

Furthermore, new evidence has shown that there is good reason for those who do not already eat bamboo to add it to their diet. Young bamboo shoots have been a food source in China for more than 2,500 years, and bamboo is much consumed throughout countries where it grows native. Young bamboo shoots are rich in nutrient compon-ents, mainly proteins, carbohydrates, minerals and fibre, and are low in fat and sugar.[33] Specifically, fresh shoots are a good source of thiamine, niacin, vitamins A, B6 and E, potassium, calcium, mangan-ese, zinc, copper, iron and chromium, and contain seventeen different amino acids, eight of which are essential for human health. Another component in bamboo shoots are phytosterols, phytonutrients that are similar to cholesterol yet have been shown to inhibit the absorp-tion of cholesterol in the intestinal tract and help lower 'bad' LDL (low-density lipoprotein) cholesterol. Currently bamboo fibre is added to many foods, including baked goods, sauces, pasta, snacks and breakfast cereals.[34]

A traditional Thai recipe: rice cooked in a bamboo culm.

By the same token, using bamboo leaves and stems as fodder for animals can help meet their nutritional needs. Bamboo has long been used for animal forage in parts of Asia, and is increasingly being supplied for a wide range of mammals in captivity throughout the world. The preliminary results of ongoing research in this area, begun in the 1990s in Oregon and Washington, USA, show favourable outcomes in comparison with grass hay.[35]

Environmental Applications

In the man-made landscape, bamboo can improve the environment in a variety of practical ways. Certain species can assist in soil stabilization and erosion control on roadway medians and embankments. Bamboo's success in controlling soil erosion is due to its extensive rhizome system. Due to this quality the material is also useful in watershed management and other hydrological functions.[36] Bamboo acts as a biofilter, providing purification of soils, water and air. It can also be used to buffer traffic noise, screen out undesirable views and control pedestrian traffic patterns. With correct planting, it can form greenbelts that act as highly effective windscreens.

All over the world, there are previously industrial areas unfit for agriculture because of high levels of contamination in the soil. In spite of this pollution, some of these areas offer enormous potential in terms of the growth of biofuels, linked to a simultaneous clean-up of the soil. Most methods of decontaminating large areas require advanced technology and are very costly. An alternative method, phytoremediation, can be less expensive, but has the disadvantage of taking a considerable time to clear the contamination. A large-scale phytoremediative effort could use bamboo as a bioaccumulator of heavy metals, while producing high biomass in response to established agricultural management.[37]

The creative harnessing of such an ecosystem is the most energy-efficient approach to air filtration, providing a market for carbon credits.[38] A carbon credit effectively allows a company or other organization to emit a certain amount of carbon dioxide into the atmosphere. A positive aspect of carbon-credit investments is that they are not only profitable, but many people consider them one of the most ethical and socially responsible investments in the world.[39] More research is needed to establish the true potential of bamboo as a means of offsetting carbon, but what is already known about its ability to sequester carbon is encouraging.[40] Bamboo can serve a role as a carbon sink, through its ability to absorb carbon dioxide and release oxygen. Bamboo charcoal used as a soil enhancer in agriculture also delivers a 'carbon-negative' system by sequestering the carbon. Recently the discovery of the formation of long-lasting phytoliths ('plant stones' made from decayed plant material) with a high carbon content in old bamboo stands also indicated a natural process of carbon sequestration.[41] Prolonged sequestration of carbon can be achieved through the huge variety of bamboo products ranging from timber to pulp.[42] Indeed, bamboo can play an important role in other ways of confronting climate change. Bamboo can contribute to the effort to keep the percentage of carbon dioxide in the atmosphere at an acceptable level, and at the same time improve the welfare of a local population by providing it with

Young plants via tissue-culture propagation of bamboos at Oprins Plants NV, Belgium.

shelter and income.[43] Bamboo provides livelihoods via the cultivation and production of goods, as well as important environmental mechanisms such as soil-erosion control, watershed maintenance and biodiversity. No other plant has the ability to interrelate ecological, social and industrial functions, including purification of soil, water and air, the creation of a green economy, the localization of renewable products and the establishment of a secure sustainable energy source.

Communities across the planet have been cultivating and harvesting bamboo for hundreds of years, from single clumps outside temples to managed forests for entire villages. Bamboo propagation techniques have improved dramatically over the past two decades, enabling young plants to be grown in large volumes for landscape applications (remedial and ornamental) and agroforestry needs,[44] with the resulting cultivation available for profitable harvesting as a wood substitute, energy source, or local use for making handicrafts. The promotion of bamboo in construction, manufacturing and energy, and as a sustainable carbon sequestration tool, could create new opportunities for agroforestry and for mitigating climate change, and improve and protect millions of rural livelihoods through investment in sustainable bamboo management, industry and technology.

The beneficial insect the praying mantis, living among bamboo. Praying mantises are carnivores, eating destructive insects that live on plants. Thier presence is considered an indication of an ecosystem in balance.

five

The Environment

There is something innately intriguing about bamboo. Indeed, there seems to be increasing global interest in bamboo for a variety of reasons: its vast distribution across diverse climatic zones, its many distinctive growth patterns and flowering systems, its ecological importance, and the range of uses and values it has for humans. Where bamboo exists naturally, it is a vital component in forest ecosystems. It serves a significant role in ecosystem dynamics within the forest through its peculiar life cycle of mass flowering and die-off.[1] But bamboo habitats are under threat, as human activities have increasingly begun to affect forests and the species living within them. Many animal species dependent on bamboos are suffering as they struggle to adapt and survive.

The World Wildlife Fund chose the giant panda (*Ailuropoda melanoleuca*) as its logo in the 1980s due to the fact that it was under threat of extinction. The panda logo represents the plight of all endangered animals, and acts as a symbol of hope that through international cooperation they can be saved. The giant panda's natural habitat has been reduced and the animal's ability to move beyond human-established borders in search of food is now extremely limited.

The only place in the world where this animal lives naturally is in the mountainous regions of western China. Extensive research has shown that there are barely 1,000 giant pandas alive at present.[2] Once this creature roamed vast areas of southeastern China, covering an area of more than a million square miles from Shanghai to Hong Kong,

The beloved giant panda enjoying a meal of bamboo.

west into Myanmar and north almost to Beijing. Pandas were sought out and hunted as prizes; even Theodore Roosevelt Jr (son of the U.S. president) shot and killed one in 1928, becoming known as the first white man to kill a giant panda.[3]

The giant panda feeds mainly on bamboo shoots, culms, branches and leaves. Because of the fibrous nature and nutritional content of bamboo, the panda needs to consume very large quantities, up to 15 kilograms (40 pounds) daily.[4] It does not store food, or hibernate, but eats all day, all year round. In its native habitat, the giant panda grazes on bamboos of 31 different species belonging to eight genera.[5] The fossilized teeth of giant pandas from three million years ago are quite similar to the teeth of the giant panda of today, indicating that the relationship between pandas and bamboo has always existed.[6] A fascinating adaptation between the giant panda and bamboo is the presence of a small, elongated bone, the radial sesamoid, located on the panda's wrists. This functions as an opposable 'thumb', complete with a set of muscles for moving it independently of the true digits.[7] Not only can the giant panda hold a bamboo stalk in one paw, but it can also pick up small twigs or even a single straw, suggesting that it has evolved to eat bamboo over a long period.

Although bamboo is a flowering plant, it primarily reproduces itself by sending up new shoots from the base of mature plants. Typically the flowering cycle can be quite long, anywhere from 15 to 120 years, according to the species.[8] When flowering occurs, most of the plants in the locale bloom at the same time and subsequently die, leaving the next generation to grow up from seed. No one can say for sure why these massive die-offs happen, but their effect on the giant panda is profound.

During the bamboo flowering period of the mid-1970s, about 2,000 square miles of bamboo were affected throughout the Min Mountains of northern Sichuan and southern Gansu.[9] Such widespread flowering had last been observed and recorded in the same area in the mid-1880s by Russian botanist M. Berezovski.[10] In 1983, during George Schaller's extensive study of the giant panda, he reported bamboo blooming in synchrony, all below the elevation of 8,500 feet. Above this elevation, the bamboo flowered and died in 1976. Different flowering cycles at different elevations help explain how pandas have been able to survive the periodic bamboo die-offs; the giant panda can simply shift up or down a slope to find food. In other areas, as many as thirteen bamboo species live simultaneously; this diversity of bamboo assures the giant panda a food supply even if some species become unavailable during mass die-offs.[11]

Bamboo seeds need the moist coolness of a forest canopy to germinate. Vulnerable to strong sun, hillsides logged for timber become too dry and seeds die. Therefore, logging, even though it may

overleaf: A sculpture by bamboo artist Jiro Yonezawa hanging in the trees at Bamboo Garden in Oregon, 2005.

not eliminate bamboo directly, ultimately deprives giant pandas of their food supply when the bamboo fails to regenerate sufficiently after a mass die-off.[12]

The giant panda is just one of many creatures dependent on bamboo. Saving natural bamboo ecosystems globally is about improving and protecting life on Earth not just for humans, but for a vast array of animal species. Extinction brought about by natural causes is an age-old process, but extinction brought about by humankind is different, and disturbing. The question is whether we are willing to admit to and confront the realities of our impact on the planet.[13]

The natural distribution of the golden monkey (*Rhinopithecus roxellana*) of Sichuan is almost identical to that of the giant panda, and so is its fate. It actually competes with the giant panda for habitat and food, and its native range is fragmented, further threatening its survival.[14] The golden monkey has a diet that consists primarily of young bamboo leaves, bamboo shoots, fruits, invertebrates, flowers and shrubs. It is an opportunistic feeder – bamboo tends to be the most frequently eaten plant because it is often available year-round – but deforestation and bamboo removal are seriously affecting the golden monkey's survival prospects.

The Himalayan black bear (*Ursus thibetanus* syn. *Selenarctos thibetanus*) is from a similar region of China. Although it often lives among bamboo forests, and is primarily an omnivore, this animal tends to feed on bamboo only in the springtime, when new shoots are available.[15] Habitat loss due to logging and the expansion of human settlements, road networks and hydropower stations, combined with hunting for skins, paws (considered a delicacy in certain quarters) and especially gall bladders (used in traditional Chinese and Korean medicines), are the main threats to this species.[16]

A distant relative of the giant panda is the red panda (*Ailurus fulgens*), found in Bhutan, China, India and Nepal. The red panda is much smaller than the giant panda, with coloration of reddish-brown with white accents. The population of these animals is also in jeopardy: there are less than 2,500 individuals in the world, including those in captivity. Typically they prefer specific species of bamboo found within their native range.[17]

The smallest known bat (*Tylonycteris parchupus*) has the nickname 'lesser bamboo bat', and is distributed from India to the Andaman Islands, including Myanmar, Thailand, Malaysia, Indonesia and the Philippines,[18] as well as throughout southern China and Hong Kong. It roosts between the nodes of mature bamboo (such as *Gigantochloa scortechinii* throughout Hong Kong). Amazingly small (around 4 cm or 1.6 in in length), it enters the bamboo culm through holes created by beetles. It is also known as the bumblebee bat and weighs approximately 1.5 grams, only slightly more than a paper clip. The lesser bamboo bat forages along pathways through bamboo forests and over their canopies.[19]

Elsewhere in the Pacific region, it is believed that there are fifteen Asian birds which live almost exclusively in bamboo; many of these are rare, and many threatened birds use bamboo as a significant portion of their habitat.[20] One example is the green-faced parrot finch (*Erythrura viridifacies*) endemic to the Philippines. It is closely associated with flowering or seeding bamboos, which are a key component of its diet.

Habitat destruction is the main threat to this beautiful bright green songbird, as it is dependent on a spatially and temporally patchy resource (bamboo seeds) within the forest. Although it benefits from initial forest disturbance, which improves the condition of the bamboo, subsequent forest clearance removes its food sources.[21]

The East African antelope the mountain bongo (*Tragelaphus eurycerus* ssp. *isaaci*) relies on bamboo thickets (*Yushania alpina*) for food and shelter during the dry season in Kenya's Aberdare Mountains. Unfortunately, due to human encroachment, the eastern mountain bongo is categorized as Endangered. The conservation of these bamboo forests is vital to protect this animal from extinction.[22]

overleaf: Bamboo can only be sustainable when it is managed and harvested properly, as here on this plantation in Anji, China. Wild-collected bamboo or overharvesting can lead to environmental degradation.

The western lowland gorilla depends on a diet of bamboo shoots.

The eastern mountain gorilla (*Gorilla beringei beringei*) inhabits mountain and bamboo forests in the eastern Democratic Republic of Congo, Rwanda and southwestern Uganda. In June and November, when the bamboo is shooting, bamboo shoots can comprise up to 90 per cent of the gorilla's diet.[23] This species was declared Endangered in 2002. Human activities (including land-management decisions and even politics) can greatly challenge populations of this great ape. The eastern mountain gorilla, which lives within a three-country park (Congo, Rwanda, Uganda), eats the bamboo shoots of *Yushania alpina*. A few years ago, the Uganda Wildlife Authority (UWA) stopped the indigenous Batwa people (aka 'pygmies') from harvesting canes in the Uganda portion of the park, fearing the Batwa were taking food away from the endangered gorillas. After a few years, the bamboo responded internally and stopped shoot production (imagine a 'rule' that told the physiology of the bamboo to sit back and soak up the flow of nutrients from existing canes and save energy until existing culms died – or were cut – and opened up light gaps for new shoots). Consequently, no shoots, no gorillas; they moved onwards to Rwanda and

Congo in search of new bamboo shoots. Eco-treks for tourists paying thousands of dollars to see mountain gorillas in Uganda began to dry up. The UWA had to allow the Batwa back into the park to practice their traditional harvest, and the 'natural' cycle resumed.[24]

In Madagascar, woody bamboos are fundamental to the survival of the endemic bamboo lemurs. Three species of lemur each inhabit a different habitat in Madagascar. The grey lemur (*Hapalemur griseus*), the greater bamboo lemur (*H. simus*) and the golden bamboo lemur (*H. aureus*) all dwell in forests with a high proportion of bamboo, and various parts of the bamboo plants contribute significantly to their diets. The grey bamboo lemur eats new shoots, leaf bases and the pith of several species, while the greater bamboo lemur eats primarily the pith of only one species (*Cathariostachys madagascariensis*). The greater bamboo lemur was thought to have become extinct in 1972, but researchers working with the WWF rediscovered this amazing animal in 1986. The newest discovered species, the golden bamboo lemur, eats leaf bases and new shoots of *C. madagascariensis* and other non-woody bamboos.[25]

The Angonoka (or ploughshare) tortoise (*G. yniphora*) lives only in the bamboo forests of the drier western part of Madagascar, and sadly is one of the most endangered reptiles in the world.[26] Meanwhile, wild Asian elephants have also been severely threatened by the loss of bamboo forests. In the 1960s, thousands of acres throughout the Yunnan province of China were destroyed to create plantations for rubber trees. An area of approximately 10,000 square hectares was opened up, destroying thousands of hectares of natural bamboo forest (*Dendrocalamus membranaceus*). This was one of the most extensive natural habitats of this clumping bamboo in China, and was also the habitat and food source of the wild Asian elephant in the region.[27]

It has been estimated that between 4 and 5 per cent of all bird species that occur in the Amazon are dependent on bamboo. The uniform finch, *Haplospiza unicolor*, has its life cycle completely synchronized with the mass-seeding bamboo species of *Chusquea*, so that this finch breeds in the austral autumn rather than the austral spring.[28]

These situations are not restricted to the tropics or to less developed countries. In North America, the once-abundant canebrakes of *Arundinaria gigantea* provided food and shelter for rare species such as Bachmann's warbler (*Vermivora bachmanii*, now categorized as Critically Endangered), while the now-extinct Carolina parakeet (*Conuropsis carolinensis*) is gone forever due to habitat destruction. Scientists have postulated that it was the Carolina parakeet's inflexible breeding pattern, as much as habitat loss, which led to its demise.[29] It is speculated that this parakeet depended on the native bamboo canebrakes to trigger courtship and breeding. Since the seed production of bamboo was a non-annual event, the parakeets' dependence on it for breeding stimulation limited reproduction. When pioneer settlers cleared river bottoms of native bamboo for crops and grazing, the reproduction of the Carolina parakeet was greatly reduced. This proximal cause of eventual extinction of the Carolina parakeet was set in motion by the wider ultimate causes, such as habitat destruction caused by logging for fuel wood and land-clearing for agriculture. John James Audubon wrote in 1844 that 'there is not now half the number that existed fifteen years ago'.[30]

Such avian species are known as 'bamboo specialists', and other examples from around the world have been documented. Andrew Kratter of the Florida Museum of Natural History has revealed nineteen bird species that are restricted to living in the thickets of bamboo (*Guadua weberbaueri*) in the lowland forests of southeastern Peru.[31] These were defined as bamboo specialists, while an additional seven species were found to show a preference for such thickets, though they also used other habitats. Species defined as bamboo specialists are also divided into subcategories. These include obligate bamboo specialists – those birds restricted entirely to these bamboo thickets throughout their entire geographic range (Kratter documented at least four such species); near-obligate bamboo specialists – birds which may use other habitats sparingly away from southeastern Peru (Kratter listed nine); and facultative bamboo specialists – those that are frequent users of habitats lacking bamboo away

Harunobu Suzuki, *Takema no uguisu* ('bush warbler in bamboo'), showing two young women gathering plants and listening to the song of the warbler amid the bamboo, 1770, woodblock print.

from southeastern Peru (Kratter found four). Such studies indicate the evolutionary habitat preference of some birds for bamboo thickets.[32] Increased human activities (agricultural and other disturbances) fragment these forests and the birds dependent on them. Conservation of bamboo forests helps protect these birds.

Aside from specialists, there are also opportunists. As mentioned, the massive die-offs of bamboo following mass flowering lead to instability in ecosystem dynamics, threatening animals and humans living nearby. In South America, *ratadas* are rodent irruptions or outbreaks that have been recorded since the Spanish conquest in the sixteenth century.[33] *Ratadas* are associated with bamboo blooming, since the increase in the availability of food (bamboo seeds) leads to an explosion in rat reproduction rates; *ratadas* are also associated with rainfall peaks. It has been documented that different species of South American bamboo have varying bloom cycles; for example, *Merostachys fistulosa* flowers every 30 years, *Chusquea quila* and/or *valdiviensis* every twelve years and some forms of *C. coleou* every fourteen years. The tendency of rats to overpopulate during these *ratadas* can lead to the spread of disease – because of this, reliable bamboo flowering predictions are needed to prevent potential epidemics.[34]

In Southeast Asia, the bamboo species *Melocanna baccifera* blossoms en masse approximately every 48 years – this is sometimes thought to be folklore but it is actually a historical and biological fact.[35] This particular type of bamboo grows throughout a large area of northeast India (primarily in the states of Mizoram and Manipur); as well as regions of Myanmar (mainly Chin State) and Bangladesh (Hill Tracts). It densely covers valleys and hillsides in the typically rugged terrain of the region. The blossoming bamboo produces a large fruit, then dies off. The fruit has a large seed, resembling an avocado, and is packed with protein and other nutrients. During the fruiting stage of the cycle, local species of forest rat feed on the bamboo fruits/seeds. The rats cease cannibalizing their young (otherwise their own way of controlling their population) and begin to reproduce in an accelerated birth surge, producing a new rat generation as often as every three months. Once the burgeoning population of rats has stripped the forest of bamboo fruits/seeds, rat swarms quietly invade farms and villages at night to devour crops and stored rice, other grains, potatoes and maize. The rodents often grow particularly large and can gnaw through bamboo

opposite: The large fruit of *Melocanna baccifera* in northeastern India.

In parts of northeastern India, the population of bamboo rats explodes during times of available bamboo seed.

and wood floors, walls, storage containers and granaries. In the past this phenomenon has resulted in mass starvation among the indigenous peoples of the region where *M. baccifera* bamboo grows.

Most natural environments, excluding those inhabited by humans, operate as balanced systems. One of the most remarkable studies on the intricacies of the web of life supporting bamboo was published in *Smithsonian Magazine* in 1994. Adele Conover was reporting on the discoveries of the Smithsonian Institute's entomologist Jerry Louton and biologist Raymond Bouchart of the Academy of Natural Sciences of Philadelphia, who were working along Peru's Rio Manú in June 1993. At the same time, coincidentally, Roy McDiarmid, a herpetologist, and Rex Crocroft, a Cornell University graduate student, were also in the Manú forest. The article, 'A New World Comes to Life, Discovered in a Stalk of Bamboo', gives a fascinating account of how these four scientists discovered 'a world within a world', a seemingly self-contained ecosystem whose existence owes itself to a shoot of bamboo (*Guadua weberbaueri*) and a nondescript brown insect (a katydid).[36]

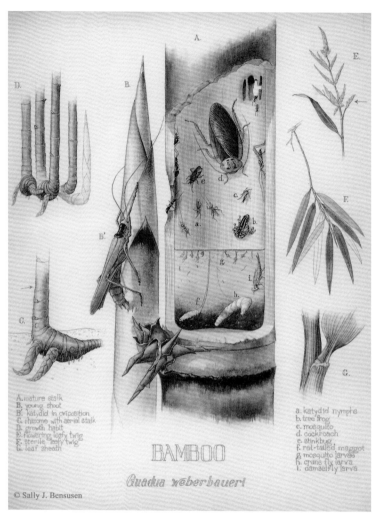

The web of life inside a bamboo culm in Peru.

The story unfolds this way: a young bamboo shoot elongates skyward, emerging from the leaf litter of a Peruvian forest floor. A brown katydid alights on the shoot and repeatedly inserts her long, knife-like ovipositor to deposit disc-shaped eggs into the shoot, 'like dimes into a piggy bank'.[37] As the great bamboo culm rapidly telescopes upwards, the stems lengthen and the tiny slits created by the katydid stretch too; the strips between the slits begin to look like bars of a tiny jail. The bamboo culm is segmented, and as it elongates, it becomes a series of hollow cavities called internodes. Within each, water accumulates in tiny pools. Eventually other creatures find these openings, and soon at least seventeen species of mosquito larvae are competing for the space. Now come larger carnivores into the pool; a damselfly hovers by and also oviposits her eggs, the rat-tailed maggot and crane-fly larvae and, eventually, the yellow-striped poison dart frog the size of a quarter slip in and out of this aerial pond. The males of this species are responsible for parental care of their young, so tadpoles ride on their fathers' backs and join the party. The aerial pond has become a microcosm, and scientists Louton and Bouchard identified 29 different aquatic insect species inhabiting the *Guadua* bamboo pond.[38]

As time passes, a number of larger animals seem also to rely on the *Guadua* and its interior pools for sustenance, including the Amazon bamboo rat, the rufous-headed woodpecker, two other birds, the Peruvian recurvebill and red-billed scythebill, and at least one species of snake. Once the bamboo has reached its maturity in height (9–18 metres or 30–60 feet), the hidden pools become food for the brown capuchin monkey (*Cebus* sp.), which grabs the culm of the bamboo in its teeth, just above the opening, and strips it downwards, like a banana peel, unzipping it for nearly a foot and exposing vulnerable creatures living within.[39]

This kind of research underscores the need to study further the environment on both a bigger and smaller scale, looking closely at the world of microcosms where ecodiversity hides and thrives. Understanding evolutionary relationships and the interconnectedness of all living things holds the key to the survival of so many creatures, big and small.

Despite the threat posed by humans to bamboo ecosystems and the animals dependent upon them, many indigenous communities consider bamboo a vital part of their daily lives. In the South Pacific region, in Papua New Guinea, tribal communities use bamboo stems as sacred receptacles for the preservation of the feathers of special birds essential to their elaborate traditional ceremonies, such as the Goroka

Life among the bamboo in Peru.

dance.[40] Gorgeously coloured feathers of several species of bird-of-paradise (Paradisaeidae) are used to adorn dancers during traditional celebrations. The respect for the life of these birds by the indigenous people is critical to the birds' preservation; hunting is tightly controlled by the tribal groups, and the birds' habitat is protected. The traditional feather adornments are passed down through three to four generations and kept in good condition in the bamboo tubes.[41]

145

Conservation of biodiversity is a necessary step towards solving the problems of poverty alleviation and sustainable development.[42] Forests are destroyed in order to make way for economic crops, such as rubber, palm oil, pineapples, bananas and fast-growing timber like teak. In other regions of natural bamboo forests, neglect and improper management has led to the decline and loss of species. Politics plays a hand as well, particularly in relation to timber regulations, land-management issues, corruption and greed. Classified in many countries as a 'non-timber forestry product', bamboo is not routinely included in resource inventories, whether agricultural or forest related.[43]

Ironically, both bamboo and animals are potentially at risk if they depend upon forest habitat for survival. Careful analysis, immediate management and proper implementation of appropriate conservation methods are needed to ensure the continued survival of both the biodiversity of bamboos and the animals dependent upon them.

Overall, the major issue for biodiversity is how its conservation may be integrated with other needs of society. The perspective that biodiversity reflects optional and intrinsic values, to be balanced with other values, appears to be compatible with the broader discipline of conservation biology, a field of study rooted in a philosophy of stewardship rather than one of utilitarianism or consumption.[44] The latter has been the basis of traditional resource conservation, or conserving resources solely because of their economic use and human consumption.[45] American philosopher J. Baird Callicott pioneers the philosophical arguments regarding non-utilitarian value and concludes that there is no easy argument to be made except a moral one: that species have some intrinsic value, and there is an ethical obligation to protect biodiversity.[46]

Biodiversity has been under threat since time immemorial, as the forces of evolutionary adaptation remain constant. Whether a species deserves to survive and live undisturbed is not the question. Every species deserves to play out its own destiny according to its own capabilities; deserves to live or die in its own way, on its own merits.[47] But when an appealing species declines due to the activities

Bamboo plantations are often found on slopes for improved drainage and as a crop that stabilizes erosion.

of humans, our very morals are challenged. The global infatuation with the plight of the giant panda is a good example. It combines both the best and worst in the complex relationship between wildlife and humankind. It would seem that any animal whose plight raises awareness of a wider issue represents a step in the right direction, but would we be so alarmed if the threatened species were a minnow or an obscure tree? The giant panda situation sets a trap in which the consequences is a loss of perspective.[48] Instead of sending costly panda ambassadors to zoos around the world, why not spend the funds on preserving the native habitat of the panda where a healthy population could sustain itself and thrive? In so doing, not only would the giant panda survive, as it has for millions of years, but all the plants within its ecosystems would endure, and its biodiversity would remain intact.

The legendary symbolism entwining bamboo and man again comes to mind. In Chinese and Japanese literature bamboo is often

overleaf: left, Colourful and bold, a new shoot of tropical *Bambusa* 'Wamin'. *right*, Damyang is synonymous with bamboo in Korea. This small town near Gwangju has a variety of bamboo forests and is home to the country's bamboo handicraft production.

seen to represent exemplary human behaviour, nobleness, gentleman-liness. Perhaps we can bring this characteristic to life through enabling bamboo to correct the destruction humans have wrought on the environment. Could bamboo truly become a protector against defilement, as suggested in the old folktales?

Leaving the forests and open space, bamboo has evolved from its primitive beginnings into a group of highly specialized grasses.[49] Adapting complex reproductive strategies and peculiar mechanisms for inhabiting niches in diverse ecosystems, bamboo continues to inspire awe and deserves respect. Bamboo may hold viable solutions for economic development while offering alternative energy sources and improving the environment – not only for us, but for all creatures on the planet.

A young bamboo –
how tall it has grown,
without the slightest help in the world.
JAPANESE HAIKU

Woodblock print diptych by Kawanabe Kyosai (1831–89), Japan.

Timeline

55–70 MYA	Bamboos begin to evolve as grasses in tropical lowlands
65 MYA	Dinosaurs become extinct
26 MYA	Fossils indicate bamboo was native in Europe (Poland)
4 MYA	Early human ancestors rise to stand on two legs
5000 BC	First reference to bamboo in Indian literature, Rigveda, 8,55,3: 'Bestow upon us a hundred bamboo clumps . . .'
1250 BC	Late Shang period, bamboo strips for writing upon to create books
500 BC	Confucius develops the game Mahjong, which uses tiles made of bamboo
400 BC	Ctesias' writings mention bamboo
200 BC	Bamboo kites used in China for military signalling
3rd century BC	Chinese paintings depict people playing bamboo instruments
2nd century BC	Tsai Lun invents paper using fibres from bamboo
AD c. 23–79	Pliny cites the first mention of bamboo in literature, from a letter by Alexander the Great to Aristotle, in his *Natural History*

311	A Chinese Buddhist writes about crossing over a bamboo bridge during his trek to India
552	Eggs of the silkworm are smuggled in a bamboo staff from China to Constantinople by two Persian monks
mid-700s	Wang Wei is one of the first Tang Dynasty artists to use bamboo in his paintings and poetry
10th century	Fireworks first appear in China during the Song Dynasty (960–1279); these are made of sticks of bamboo packed with gunpowder
1037–1101	Poet Su-Shi (Dongpo) writes about bamboo
1200	Marco Polo brings gunpowder packed in bamboo back to Europe
1649	Japanese ordinance mandates that peasants must plant bamboo in order to use the leaves as fuel
1679	*Manual of the Mustard Seed*, a Chinese painting manual, gives instructions on how to paint bamboo
1736	*Phyllostachys pubescens* (moso) is imported from China to Japan by Yoshitaka Shimadzu. Now the most widely cultivated bamboo throughout Japan
1753	*Species Plantarum* is published: *Arundo bambus* cited by Carl Linnaeus
1787–1861	Lifetime of Ema Saiko, Japanese poet of kanshi and exquisite painter of bamboo
1855	Eugene Mazel plants bamboo and other exotics to develop what will become the park Le Bambouseraie de Prafrance, near Anduze, France
1827	*Phyllostachys nigra*, black bamboo, arrives in England from Japan
1830s–1850s	Vast areas of native canebrake in North America are destroyed through land clearing by European settlers

1868	Publication of the *Monograph on the Bambusaceae* by William Munro, London
1880	Edison continues to improve his light bulb until it can last for over 1,200 hours, using a bamboo-derived filament collected in Japan
1882	*Phyllostachys aurea*, an ornamental bamboo, is introduced to America via China
1896	Publication date of A. B. Freeman-Mitford's book *The Bamboo Garden*
1901	Bamboo aircraft flight, Gustave Whitehead Fairfield, Connecticut, USA
1903	Edmund 'Chinese' Wilson discovers 'umbrella bamboo' in the wilds of China and names the species after his daughter Muriel
1906	Jean Houzeau De Lahaie publishes periodical bulletin *Le Bambou Son Etude, Sa Culture, Son Emploi*, promoting bamboo planting in Belgium and France
1914	Charlie Chaplin adopts 'tramp' costume with bamboo cane
1945	Bamboo survives the atomic bomb explosion in Hiroshima, Japan
1958–1960	*Mautum* – mass flowering and die-off of *Melocanna baccifera* in northeast India, resulting in starvation and civil unrest
1960	Koichiro Ueda publishes *Studies of the Physiology of Bamboo*
1960	'House of Bamboo' performed by Earl Grant, written by Bill Crompton and Norman Murrells, the Number One hit song in the U.S. pop charts
1966	Publication of *Bamboo: A Fresh Perspective* by Floyd McClure, leading to renewed interest in bamboo research

1970s	*Fargesia murieliae* (umbrella bamboo) flowering and mass die-off in the giant panda region of China
1980s	World Wildlife Fund adopts China's giant panda as logo
1981	First use of bamboo in modern-day ethanol production
1984	David Farrelly publishes *The Book of Bamboo*, leading to a revival of bamboo enthusiasm among environmentalists
1993	First laminated bamboo flooring and plywood products appear in Western markets
1998	Bamboo aerocraft Flyboo on display in Paris, France
1999	Success of Gielis and Oprins in in-vitro micro-propagation of temperate bamboos leads to major breakthroughs in bamboo's horticulture and forestry potential
2000	Gunther Pauli's ZERI bamboo pavilion at EXPO 2000: Germany showcases bamboo's uses in modern architecture
2002	*Masters of Bamboo*, a Lloyd. E. Cotsen collection of bamboo vessels celebrating the elevated art of bamboo weaving, is donated to the Asian Art Museum in San Francisco, California
2009	First annual World Bamboo Day announced by the government of Thailand

Appendix 1: Tribes and Subtribes of Bamboo

Tribe Bambuseae refers to the tropical woody bamboos, and comprises around 1,000 species, distributed into nine subtribes, and around 91 genera:

Bambuseae include the following subtribes:

1 Subtribe Arthrostylidiinae (Neotropical)
2 Subtribe Bambusinae (Paleotropical)
3 Subtribe Chusqueinae (Neotropical)
4 Subtribe Guaduinae (Neotropical)
5 Subtribe Melocanninae (Paleotropical)
6 Subtribe Hickeliinae (Paleotropical)
7 Subtribe Racemobambosinae (Paleotropical)

1. Subtribe Arthrostylidiinae

Comprises 12 genera:

Actinocladum *Elytrostachys*
Alvimia *Filgueirasia*
Arthrostylidium *Glaziophyton*
Athroostachys *Merostachys*
Atractantha *Myriocladus*
Aulonemia (*Matudacalamus*) *Rhipidocladum*
Colanthelia

2. Subtribe Bambusinae

Comprises 21 genera:

Bambusa (Dendrocalamopsis)
Bonia (Monocladus)
Dendrocalamus (Klemachloa, Sinocalamus)
Dinochloa
Fimbribambusa
Gigantochloa
Holttumochloa
Kinabaluchloa
Maclurachloa
Melocalamus
Neololeba

Neomicrocalamus
Oreobambos
Oxytenanthera
Pinga
Soejatmia
Sphaerobambos
Temburongia
Temochloa
Thyrsostachys
Vietnamosasa

3. Subtribe Chusqueinae

Comprises one genus:

Chusquea (Dendragrostis, Rettbergia, Neurolepsis, Planotia)

4. Subtribe Guaduinae

Comprises five genera:

Apoclada
Eremocaulon (Criciuma)
Guadua

Olmeca
Otatea

5. Subtribe Melocanninae

Comprises nine genera:

Cephalostachyum
Davidsea
Melocanna (Beesha)
Neohouzeaua
Ochlandra
Pseudostachyum
Schizostachyum (Leptocanna)
Stapletonia
Teinostachyum

6. Subtribe Hickeliinae

Comprises nine genera:

Cathariostachys
Decaryochloa
Greslania
Hickelia
Hitchcockella
Nastus
Perrierbambus
Sirochloa
Valiha

7. Subtribe Racemobambodinae

Comprises one genus:

Racemobambos

✦

Tribe Arundinarieae refers to the temperate woody bamboos

Comprises 24 genera:

Acidosasa	*Indosasa*
Ampelocalamus	*Oligostachyum*
Arundinaria	*Phyllostachys*
Brachystachyum	*Pseudosasa*
Chimonobambusa	*Qiongzhuea* (now usually included in
Chimonocalamus (*Sinarundinaria*)	*Chimonobambusa*)
Drepanostachyum	*Sasa*
Fargesia (includes *Borinda*)	*Semiarundinaria*
Ferrocalamus	*Shibataea*
Gaoligongshania	*Sinobambusa*
Gelidocalamus	*Thamnocalamus*
Himalayacalamus	*Yushania*
Indocalamus	

Tribe Olyreae refers to the herbaceous (non-woody) bamboos and includes about 120 species, which are often divided into three subtribes

SOURCE: Bamboo Phylogeny Group, directed by Lynn G. Clark,
Iowa State University, USA, 2012

Appendix II: Bamboo Gardens and Arboreta

Europe

La Bambouseraie de Prafrance, Anduze, France

Benmore, satellite garden of Edinburgh Botanical Garden, Scotland

Bokrijk Arboretum, Limburg, Belgium

Carwinion, Cornwall, UK

Logan, satellite garden of Royal Botanical Garden, Edinburgh, Scotland

Ness Botanical Gardens, Liverpool, UK

Palmengarten, Frankfurt, Germany

Royal Botanical Garden Edinburgh, Scotland

Royal Botanical Gardens, Kew, Richmond, UK

Wakehurst Place, West Sussex, UK

Wisley Royal Horticultural Society Garden, Surrey, UK

North and South America

Bamboo Farm and Coastal Gardens, Savannah, Georgia, USA

Campinas, Instituto Agronomico, Brazil

Fairchild Tropical Gardens, Coral Gables, Florida, USA

Huntington Botanical Gardens, Pasadena, California, USA

Jungle Gardens, Avery Island, Louisiana, USA

Longwood Gardens, Kennett Square, Pennsylvania, USA

National Zoo, Washington, DC, USA

New York Botanical Gardens, Bronx, New York, USA

Rip van Winkle Gardens, Jefferson Island, Louisiana, USA

San Diego Botanical Gardens (aka Quail Gardens), Encinitas, California, USA

São Paulo Botanical Gardens, Brazil

Asia

Anji Bamboo Museum Garden, China

Bogor Botanical Garden, Java, Indonesia

Damyang Bamboo Park, South Jeolla Province, South Korea

Fuji Bamboo Gardens, Mishima, Japan

Fushan Botanical Garden, Taiwan

Hong Kong Botanical Gardens, China

Juknokwon, Damyang, South Korea

Koishikawa Botanical Garden, Tokyo, Japan

Minamata Memorial Garden, Minamata, Japan

Rakusai Bamboo Gardens, Kyoto, Japan

Shanghai Botanical Garden, China

Singapore Botanical Gardens, Singapore

Taipei Botanical Garden, Taiwan

Toyama Botanical Gardens, Japan

World Horticultural Expo Garden, Kunming, Yunnan, China

References

Introduction

1 International Network of Bamboo and Rattan, *Socio-economic Constraints in the Bamboo and Rattan Sectors, Inbar's Assessment*, Working Paper no. 23 (1999), p. 1.

2 Food and Agriculture Organization of the United Nations (FAO), *Global Forest Resources Assessment* (Rome, 2005), p. 29.

3 Yuji Isagi, 'Carbon Stock and Cycling in a Bamboo *Phyllostachys bambusoides* Stand', *Ecological-Research*, IX/1 (1994), p. 42.

4 Adele Conover and Sally J. Bensusen, 'A New World Comes to Life, Discovered in a Stalk of Bamboo', *Smithsonian Magazine*, XXV/7 (1994), pp. 120–28.

5 Emmet Judziewicz, Lynn G. Clark, Ximena Londono and Margaret J. Stern, *American Bamboos* (Washington, DC, 1999), p. 77.

6 David G. Fairchild, *The World Grows Round My Door* (New York, 1947), p. 57.

7 See the International Network of Bamboo and Rattan website, www.inbar.int, accessed 18 April 2011.

8 G. Brundtlant et al., 'Our Common Future', in *Report of the 1987 World Commission on Environmental Development* (Oxford, 1987), p. 43.

9 Mathis Wackernagel and William Rees, *Our Ecological Footprint: Reducing Human Impact on the Earth* (Gabriola Island, BC, 1996), p. 9.

10 Lou Yiping et al., *Bamboo and Climate Change Mitigation in International Network of Bamboo and Rattan Technical Report No. 32* (China, 2011), p. 9.

11 International Organization for Standardization, No. 14040 (Geneva, 1997).

12 John Elkington, *Cannibals with Forks: The Triple Bottom Line of the 21st Century Business* (Oxford, 1997), p. 1.

13 Judziewicz et al., *American Bamboos*, p. 76.

14 Chief Justice Warren Burger, *Tennessee Valley Authority v. Hill, 437 U.S. 153* (Washington, DC, 1978).

References

1 Distribution, Diversity and Classification

1   Lynn G. Clark, personal communication, 2011.
2   Chris M. A. Stapleton et al., 'Molecular Phylogeny of Asian Woody Bamboos: Review for the Flora of China', *Science and Culture: The Journal of the American Bamboo Society*, XXII/1 (2009), p. 14.
3   Elżbieta Worobiec and Grzegorz Worobiec, 'Leaves and Pollen of Bamboos from the Polish Neogene', *Review of Palaeobotany and Palynology*, CXXXIII/1–2 (2005), pp. 39–50.
4   P. Shanmughavel, K. Francis and M. George, *Plantation Bamboo* (Dehra Dun, India, 1997), p. 15.
5   Ibid., p. 16.
6   Yulong Ding et al., 'Anatomical Studies on the Rhizome of Monopodial Bamboos', International Union of Forest Research Organizations Division 5 conference proceedings (1993), p. 759.
7   I. V. Ramanuja Rao, 'Bamboos and their Role in Ecosystem Rehabilitation', in *Encyclopedia of Forest Sciences*, ed. Julian Evans, John A. Youngquist and Jeffrey Burley (Oxford, 2005), vol. III, pp. 1011–16.
8   Emmet Judziewicz, Lynn G. Clark, Ximena Londono and Margaret J. Stern, *American Bamboos* (Washington, DC, 1999), p. 67.
9   Ibid., p.64.
10 Nadia Bystriakova and Valerie Kapos, 'Bamboo Diversity – The Need for a Red List Review', *Biodiversity*, VI/4 (2006), p. 14.
11 Lynn G. Clark, Bamboo Biodiversity website, www.eeob.iastate.edu/research/bamboo, accessed January 2013.
12 Ibid.
13 F. Fijten, 'A Taxonomic Revision of *Buergersiochloa* Pilger (Gramineae)', *Blumea*, XXII (1975), pp. 415–18.
14 Clark, Bamboo Biodiversity website.
15 Emmet Judziewicz and L. G. Clark, in press.
16 Clark, Bamboo Biodiversity website.
17 Ibid.
18 Ibid.
19 Ra. Rao, 'Bamboos and their Role in Ecosystem Rehabilitation', pp. 1011–16.
20 Shozo Shibata, 'Consideration of the Flowering Periodicity of *Melocanna baccifera* through Past Records and Recent Flowering with a 48-year Interval', *8th World Bamboo Congress Proceedings*, V (2009), pp. 90–95.
21 Robert Austin, Dana Levy and Koichiro Ueda, *Bamboo* (New York, 1970), p. 14.
22 P. Shanmughavel, K. Francis and M. George, *Plantation Bamboo* (Dehra Dun, India, 1997), p. 16.
23 Shibata, 'Consideration of the Flowering Periodicity of *Melocanna baccifera*', pp. 90–95.
24 Judziewicz et al., *American Bamboos*, p. 67.
25 Rao, 'Bamboos and their Role in Ecosystem Rehabilitation', pp. 1011–16.

26   Thomas R. Soderstrom, 'Bamboo Systematics: Yesterday, Today and Tomorrow', *Journal of the American Bamboo Society*, VI/1–4 (1985), pp. 4–13.

27   Thomas R. Soderstrom and R. P. Ellis, 'The Position of Bamboo Genera and Allies in a System of Grass Classification', in *Grasses: Systematics and Evolution*, ed. S.W.L. Jacobs and J. Everett (Washington, DC, 1987), pp. 225–38.

28   American Bamboo Society, www.bamboo.org, accessed 18 April 2013.

29   Lynn G. Clark, personal communication, 2011.

2 Horticulture

1   Thomas R. Soderstrom, 'Bamboo Systematics: Yesterday, Today and Tomorrow', *Journal of the American Bamboo Society*, VI/1–4 (1985), p. 9.

2   Richard Haubrich, preface to Ernest Mason Satow, *The Cultivation of Bamboos in Japan* (reprint Solana Beach, CA, 1995), p. 1.

3   Soderstrom, 'Bamboo Systematics: Yesterday, Today and Tomorrow', p. 9.

4   Ibid.

5   Koichiro Ueda, *Studies on the Physiology of Bamboo with Reference to Practical Application* (Tokyo, 1960), pp. iii–v.

6   Soderstrom, 'Bamboo Systematics: Yesterday, Today and Tomorrow', p. 10.

7   Yves Crouzet, *La Bambouseraie: History of the Bambouseraie* (Anduze, 1995), pp. 2–3.

8   American Bamboo Society website, www.bamboo.org, accessed 18 April 2013.

9   World Bamboo Organization website, www.worldbamboo.net, accessed 18 April 2013.

3 The Hand of Man

1   Tsuen Hsuin Tsien, *Written on Bamboo and Silk: The Beginnings of Chinese Books and Inscriptions* (Chicago, IL, 1962).

2   Endymion Porter Wilkinson, *Chinese History: A Manual* (Cambridge, MA, 2000), p. 445.

3   'Tibetan Artist Strives to Sustain Traditional Calligraphy', Xinhua News Agency, http://news.xinhuanet.com, 1 November 2011.

4   Robert Austin and Koichiro Ueda, *Bamboo* (New York, 1970), p. 10.

5   Mary Sisk Noguchi, 'Majestic Bamboo is Firmly Rooted in Kanji', *Japan Times*, 25 July 2011, www.japantimes.co.jp.

6   Oscar Hidalgo-Lopez, *Gift of the Gods* (Bogotá, 2003), p. 522.

7   Ibid.

8   David Farrelly, *The Book of Bamboo* (San Francisco, CA, 1984), pp. 13–69.

9   Walter Liese, *The Anatomy of Bamboo Culms*, Technical Report 18 (China, 1998), p. 35.

10   Farrelly, *The Book of Bamboo*, pp. 13–69.

11 Marcelo Villegas, *New Bamboo: Architecture and Design* (Bogotá, 2003), p. 44;
    Liese, *The Anatomy of Bamboo Culms*, pp. 161–5.
12 Ho Yin Lee and Stephen Lau, 'Bamboo Scaffolding of Hong Kong',
    Hong Kong Institute of Architects Journal, I (1995), pp. 60–64.
13 Farrelly, *The Book of Bamboo*, p. 37.
14 Liese, *The Anatomy of Bamboo Culms*, p. 162.
15 Anna Sproule, *Thomas A. Edison: The World's Greatest Inventor* (Woodbridge,
    CT, 2000).
16 Wikipedia, 'Bamboo Musical Instruments', http://en.wikipedia.org,
    accessed 18 April 2013.
17 Emmet Judziewicz, Lynn G. Clark, Ximena Londono and Margaret J.
    Stern, *American Bamboos* (Washington, DC, 1999), pp. 97–100.
18 Yuan-Yuan Lee and Sinyan Shen, *Chinese Musical Instruments*, Chinese
    Music Monograph Series (Chicago, IL, 1999)
19 Wikipedia, 'Bamboo Musical Instruments'.
20 Ibid.
21 'Jew's Harp', www.pertout.com/Jew'sHarp, accessed 18 April 2013.
22 Yamaha Corporation of America, www.yamaha.com
23 Wikipedia, 'Kau Cim', http://en.wikipedia.org, accessed 26 March 2013.
24 Stewart Culin, 'The Game of Ma-Jong, its Origin and Significance',
    Brooklyn Museum Quarterly, XI (1924), pp. 153–68.
25 'Chinlone', at www.chinlone.com, accessed 26 March 2013.
26 Saw Eh Dah, 'Bamboo and Rattan of Myanmar', INBAR Country Report
    (China, 2005).
27 Philacor Young People's Library, *Games Filipino Children Play* (Philippines,
    1978).
28 Ibid.
29 Luis Marden, *The Angler's Bamboo* (New York, 1997), pp. 1–3.
30 V. M. Patino, *Historia de la vegetación natural y de sus componentes en la America
    equinoccial* (Bogotá, 1975).
31 Ibid.
32 Mabel Cook Cole, *Philippine Folk Tales* (Chicago, IL, 1916), pp. 187–8.
33 Sir James George Frazer, *Folk-lore in the Old Testament*, vol. I of Studies in
    Comparative Religion, Legend and Law (London, 1918).
34 Fanny Hagin Mayer, trans. and ed., *The Yanagita Kunio Guide to the Japanese
    Folk Tale* (Indianapolis, IN, 1948), pp. 8–9.
35 Gertrude Jobes, *Dictionary of Mythology, Folklore, and Symbols* (New York,
    1961), pp. 177–8.
36 Mayer, *The Yanagita Kunio Guide to the Japanese Folk Tale*.
37 Jobes, *Dictionary of Mythology Folklore and Symbols* , p. 177.
38 Nancy Moore Bess, *Bamboo in Japan* (New York, 2001), p. 15.
39 Wolfram Eberhard, ed., *Folktales of China* (New York, 1973), p. 18.
40 Richard Barnhart et al., *Three Thousand Years of Chinese Painting* (New
    Haven, CT, and Beijing, 1997).
41 Alexander H. Lawson, *Bamboos: A Gardener's Guide to their Cultivation in
    Temperate Climates* (London, 1968), p. 14.

42   Thomas R. Soderstrom, 'Bamboo Systematics: Yesterday, Today and Tomorrow', *Journal of the American Bamboo Society*, VI/1–4 (1985), p. 1.

43   D. N. Tewari, *A Monograph on Bamboo* (Dehra Dun, India, 1992), p. 219.

44   P. Shanmughavel, K. Francis and M. George, *Plantation Bamboo* (Dehra Dun, India, 1997), p. 114.

45   Victor Cusack and Deidre Stewart, *Bamboo World: The Growing and Use of Clumping Bamboos* (Kenthurst, NSW, 1999), p. 176.

46   R. Rinpoche and J. Kunzang, *Tibetan Medicine* (Berkeley, CA, 1973).

47   Shanmughavel et al., *Plantation Bamboo*, p. 116.

48   Nirmala Chongtham et al., 'Nutritional Properties of Bamboo Shoots: Potential and Prospects for Utilization as a Health Food', *Comprehensive Reviews in Food Science and Food Safety*, X/3 (2011), pp. 153–68.

49   Ibid.

4 Modern Potentials, Today and Tomorrow

 1   John Marsh and Nigel Smith, 'New Bamboo Industries and Pro-Poor Impacts: Lessons from China and Potential for Mekong Countries', *A Cut for the Poor: Proceedings of the International Conference on Managing Forests for Poverty Reduction: Capturing Opportunities in Forest Harvesting and Wood Processing for the Benefit of the Poor* (Thailand, 2007), no. 20.

 2   Jules Janssen and Lou Yiping, 'Capturing Carbon with Bamboo', BAM-BOO: *The Magazine of the American Bamboo Society*, XXXI/3 (2010), p. 10.

 3   Oscar Hidalgo-Lopez, *Gift of the Gods* (Bogotá, 2003), pp. 72–97.

 4   Important research in the area includes *Studies on the Physiology of Bamboo* (1960) by Koichiro Ueda, a prominent Japanese scholar recognized as one of the leading authorities on bamboo; the work of Walter Liese, who dedicated his wood anatomy research to the study of bamboo's molecular structure; and the investigations of Jules Janssen of the University of Eindhoven, the Netherlands, who led scientific testing of tensile strengths and designed engineering strategies for modern applications rivalling traditional timber utilization.

 5   Walter Liese, *The Anatomy of Bamboo Culms*, Technical Report 18 (China, 1998), p. 7.

 6   Hidalgo-Lopez, *Gift of the Gods*, p. 240.

 7   Ibid., p. 236.

 8   Ibid., p. 174.

 9   Tristan Roberts, 'Bamboo Dimensional Lumber? *Lumboo* Is Here', in *Environmental Building News*, XIX/6 (2010), p. 1

10   Yuji Isagi, 'Carbon Stock and Cycling in a Bamboo *Phyllostachys bambusoides* stand', *Ecological-Research*, IX/1 (1994), p. 42.

11   Raimund Duking, Walter Liese and Johan Gielis, 'Carbon Flux and Carbon Stock in a Bamboo Stand and their Relevance for Mitigating Climate Change', *Bamboo Science and Culture*, XXIV/1 (2011), pp. 1–6.

12   Hidalgo-Lopez, *Gift of the Gods*, p. XV.

13   Ibid., pp. 356–63.

14 See Litrax, at www.litrax.com and SwicoFil AG, at www.swicofil.com, accessed 18 April 2013.

15 Hidalgo-Lopez, *Gift of the Gods*, pp. 164–75.

16 United States Food and Drug Administration, 'Update on Bisphenol a (BPA) for Use in Food', *Public Health Focus* (2010), pp. 1–7, at www.fda.gov.

17 See www.litrax.com.

18 Biodegradable pots at www.enviroarc.net, accessed 23 March 2013.

19 Michel Abadie, 'Human Flying and Bamboo Fiber, from the Aviation Pioneer to Contemporary Design', *8th World Bamboo Congress Proceedings* (2009), pp. 1–10.

20 Jeff Greenwald, 'Turning Bamboo into a Bicycle', *Smithsonian Magazine*, 29 June 2011, www.smithsonianmag.com.

21 Ibid.

22 Ibid.

23 Michael Temmerman, 'Bamboo Energy Yield through Combustion', paper given at conference *Bamboo: From Tradition to High Tech*, Belgium (2011).

24 T. J. Barreto de Menezes and A. Azzini, *O bambu, uma nova materia para producao de Etanol, Instituto Agronomico de Campinas* (Brazil, 1981).

25 Temmerman, 'Bamboo Energy Yield Through Combustion'.

26 See www.litrax.com.

27 I. R. Hunter, 'Bamboo Resources, Uses and Trade: The Future?', *Journal of Bamboo and Rattan*, 11/4 (2003), p. 319.

28 Jia Horng Lin et al., 'PET/PP Blend with Bamboo Charcoal to Produce Functional Composites: Evaluation of Functionalities', *Advanced Materials Research: Smart Materials*, LV–LVII (2008), p. 433.

29 Jinhe Fu, Tesfaye Hunde et al., 'Bamboo Biomass Energy: A Partnership between Ghana, Ethiopia, China and INBAR', *8th World Bamboo Congress Proceedings* (2009), pp. 1–8.

30 Darrel Miller, 'Did You Know That Bamboo Extract Is High In Silica And Good For The Skin?', www.isnare.com, accessed 23 March 2013.

31 Ibid.

32 Laura Van Hoywegeh, 'Phytochemical Analysis of Bamboo Leaves', paper given at conference *Bamboo: From Tradition to High Tech*, Belgium (2011).

33 Nirmala Chongtham et al., 'Nutritional Properties of Bamboo Shoots: Potential and Prospects for Utilization as a Health Food', Comprehensive Reviews in Food Science and Food Safety, X/3 (2011), pp. 153–68.

34 Ibid.

35 Daphne Lewis and Carol Miles, *Farming Bamboo* (Raleigh, NC, 2007), pp. 84–5.

36 P. Shanmughavel, K. Francis and M. George, *Plantation Bamboo* (Dehra Dun, India, 1997), p. 59.

37 Geert Potters et al., 'Energy Crops in Western Europe: Is Bamboo an Acceptable Alternative?', paper given at conference *Bamboo: From Tradition to High Tech*, Belgium (2011), conference proceedings, pp. 22–34.

38 S. D. Ebbs and L. V. Kochian, 'Toxicity of Zinc and Copper to Brassica
    Species: Implications for Phytoremediation', *Journal of Environmental
    Quality*, XXVI (1997), pp. 776–81.
39 Marisha Farnsworth, 'Urban Bamboo Biofilter' blog,
    http://urbanbamboobiofilter.blogspot.co.uk, accessed 18 April 2013.
40 Raimund Duking, Walter Liese and Johan Gielis, 'Carbon Flux and
    Carbon Stock in a Bamboo Stand and their Relevance for Mitigating
    Climate Change', *Bamboo Science and Culture*, XXIV/1 (2011), pp. 1–6.
41 Jeffrey Parr, Leigh Sullivan et al., 'Carbon Bio-sequestration within the
    Phytoliths of Economic Bamboo Species', *Global Change Biology*, XVI/10
    (2010), pp. 2661–7.
42 Duking et al., 'Carbon Flux and Carbon Stock in a Bamboo Stand',
    pp. 1–6.
43 Janssen and Yiping, 'Capturing Carbon with Bamboo', p. 10.
44 Harry van Trier and Jan Oprins, *Bambuseae: A Material for Landscape and
    Garden Design* (Leuven, 2004), pp. 38–49.

5 The Environment

1 Nadia Bystriakova, Valerie Kapos, Chris Stapleton and Igor Lysenko,
   *Bamboo Biodiversity: Information for Planning Conservation and Management in the
   Asia-Pacific Region* (Cambridge, 2003), p. 7.
2 George Schaller, *The Last Panda* (Chicago, IL, 1994), p. 6.
3 Michael McIntosh, 'World Enough and Time', *Wildlife Art News*, XI/2
   (1992), p. 94.
4 Ibid., p. 95.
5 Yi Tong-Pei, 'The Classification and Distribution of Bamboo Eaten by
   the Giant Panda in the Wild', *Journal of the American Bamboo Society*, VI/1–4
   (1985), p. 112.
6 Schaller, *The Last Panda*, p. 6.
7 McIntosh, 'World Enough and Time', p. 96.
8 Julian Campbell, 'Bamboo Flowering Patterns: A Global View with
   Special Reference to East Asia', *Journal of the American Bamboo Society*,
   VI/1–4 (1985), p. 17.
9 Schaller, *The Last Panda*, p. 137.
10 Dieter Ohrnberger, *The Bamboos of the World* (Amsterdam, 1999), p. 141.
11 Schaller, *The Last Panda*, p. 173.
12 Ibid., p. 212.
13 McIntosh, 'World Enough and Time', p. 96.
14 Schaller, *The Last Panda*, p. 27.
15 Ibid., p. 169.
16 International Union for Conservation of Nature and Natural Resources,
    Red List of Threatened Species, www.iucnredlist.org, accessed 18 April 2013.
17 Schaller, *The Last Panda*, p. 109.
18 University of Bristol, School of Biology, 'Lesser Bamboo Bat',
    www.bio.bris.ac.uk/research/bats, accessed 18 April 2013.

19 Gary Ades, 'Important Discovery of Lesser Bamboo Bat Roosting Site in Hong Kong', *Porcupine!*, IX (1999), p. 22.

20 BirdLife International, *Threatened Birds of the World* (Barcelona and Cambridge, 2000).

21 BirdLife International species factsheet: *Erythrura viridifacies* (2012), www.birdlife.org.

22 Antelope Taxon Advisory Group, San Diego Zoo Global Library (California, 2003), http://library.sandiegozoo.org/factsheet/pronghorn/pronghorn.htm, p. 7.

23 Royal Belgium Institute of Natural Sciences, Convention of Migratory Species Gorilla Agreement, www.naturalsciences.be (2011).

24 Paul Weatherly, Gorilla Bond, personal communication (Washington, DC, 2010).

25 Nick Garbutt, *Mammals of Madagascar* (Sante Fe, NM, 1999); R. A. Mittermeier, I. Tattersall, W. R. Konstant, D. M. Meyers and R. B. Mast, *Lemurs of Madagascar* (Washington, DC, 1994).

26 International Union for Conservation of Nature and Natural Resources, *Red List of Threatened Species*, www.iucnredlist.org, accessed 18 April 2013.

27 Yang Yuming and Hui Chaomao, eds, *China's Bamboo: Culture, Resources, Cultivation, Utilization* (Beijing, 2010), p. 217.

28 Paul D. Haemig, 'Birds and Mammals Associated with Bamboo in the Atlantic Forest', *Ecology Info*, V (2011).

29 Emmet Judziewicz, Lynn G. Clark, Ximena Londono and Margaret J. Stern, *American Bamboos* (Washington, DC, 1999), p. 77.

30 John James Audubon, 'The Carolina Parrot', in *The Birds of America* (Edinburgh and London, 1827–38), online at www.audubon.org, accessed 18 April 2013.

31 A. W. Kratter, 'Bamboo Specialization by Amazonian Birds', in *Biotropica*, XXIX (1997), pp. 100–10.

32 Ibid.

33 Fabian Jaksic and Mauricio Lima, 'Myths and Facts on Ratadas: Bamboo Blooms, Rainfall Peaks and Rodent Outbreaks in South America', *Austral Ecology*, XXVIII/3 (2003), pp. 237–51.

34 Ibid.

35 Shozo Shibata, 'Consideration of the Flowering Periodicity of *Melocanna baccifera* through Past Records and Recent Flowering with a 48-year Interval', paper given at the *8th World Bamboo Congress Proceedings*, V (2009), pp. 90–95.

36 Adele Conover and Sally J. Bensusen, 'A New World Comes to Life, Discovered in a Stalk of Bamboo', *Smithsonian Magazine*, XXV/7 (1994), pp. 120–28.

37 Ibid.

38 Ibid.

39 Ibid.

40 Miriam Supuma, 'Birds of the Gods', on *Nature*, Public Broadcasting System (2011).

41 Ibid.

42 Yuming and Chaomao, eds, *China's Bamboo*, p. 220.

43 Nadia Bystriakova, Valerie Kapos and Igor Lysenko, *Potential Distribution of Woody Bamboos in Africa and America*, Working Paper no. 43 (Cambridge, 2002), p. 1.

44 Gary K. Meffe, *Ecosystem Management: Adaptive, Community-based Conservation* (Washington, DC, 2000), p. 238.

45 Ibid.

46 J. Baird Callicott, 'The Metaphysical Implications of Ecology', *Environmental Ethics*, 8 (1986), p. 140.

47 McIntosh, 'World Enough and Time', pp. 93–9.

48 Ibid.

49 Lynn G. Clark, personal communication, 2011.

Further Reading

Austin, Robert, Dana Levy and Ueda Koichiro, *Bamboo* (New York and Tokyo, 1970)

Bell, Michael, *The Gardener's Guide to Growing Temperate Bamboos* (Portland, OR and London, 2000)

Bess, Nancy Moore, *Bamboo in Japan* (Tokyo, New York and London, 2001)

Carunchco, Eric S., *Designing Filipino: The Architecture of Francisco Manosa* (Manila, 2003)

Chen, Shou-liang and Liang-chi Chia, *Chinese Bamboos* (Beijing and Portland, OR, 1988)

Chua, K. S., B. C. Soong and H.T.W. Tan, *The Bamboos of Singapore* (Singapore, 1996)

Coffland, Robert T. and Pat Pollard, *Contemporary Japanese Bamboo Arts* (Chicago, IL, 2000)

Cusack, Victor, *Bamboo Rediscovered* (Trentham, Australia, 1998)

—, and Deirdre Stewart, *Bamboo World* (Trentham, Australia, 2000)

Dajun, Wang and Shen Shap-Jin, *Bamboos of China* (Portland, OR, 1987)

Dart, Durnford, *The Bamboo Handbook: A Farmers, Growers, and Product Developers' Guide* (Queensland, 1999)

DeBoer, Darrel, and Megan Groth, *Bamboo Building Essentials* (San Francisco, CA, 2010)

Dransfield, Soejatmi, and E. A. Widjaja, *Plant Resources of South-East Asia, 7, Bamboos* (Leiden, 1995)

—, *The Bamboos of Sabah* (Sabah, 1992)

Dunkelberg, Klaus, *IL 31 Bambus (Bamboo as a Building Material)* (Stuttgart, 1985)

Earle, Joe, *New Bamboo: Contemporary Japanese Masters* (New York, 2008)

Farrelly, David, *The Book of Bamboo* (San Francisco, CA, 1995)

Hidalgo-Lopez, Oscar, *Bamboo: The Gift of the Gods* (Bogatá, 2003)

Janssen, Jules J. A., *Building with Bamboo: A Handbook* (Eindhoven, 1995)

Judziewicz, Emmett J., Lynn G. Clark, Ximena Londoño and Margaret J. Stern, *American Bamboos* (Washington, DC, and London, 1999)

Kaley, Vinoo, *Venu Bharati: A Comprehensive Volume on Bamboo* (New Delhi, 2000)

Koshy, K. C., *Bamboos at TBGRI* (Kerala, 2010)

Lewis, Daphne and Carol Miles, *Farming Bamboo* (Seattle, WA, 2007)
——, *Hardy Bamboos for Shoots and Poles* (Seattle, WA, 1998)
Liese, Walter, *The Anatomy of Bamboo Culms* (Beijing, Eindhoven and New Delhi, 1998)
——, and Satish Kumar, *Bamboo Preservation Compendium* (New Delhi, 2003)
McClure, Floyd A., *The Bamboos: A Fresh Perspective* [1966] (Boston, MA, 1993)
Meredith, Ted Jordan, *Bamboo for Gardens* (Portland, OR, 2001)
——, *Pocket Guide to Bamboos* (Portland, OR, and London, 2009)
Ohrnberger, Dieter, *The Bamboos of the World: Annotated Nomenclature and Literature of the Species and the Higher and Lower Taxa* (Amsterdam, 1999)
Poudyal, Punya P., *Bamboos of Sikkim, Bhutan, and Nepal* (Katmandu, 2006)
Scheer, Jo, *How to Build with Bamboo: 19 Projects You Can do at Home* (Salt Lake City, UT, 2005)
Seethalakshmi, K. K., and M. S. Muktesh Kumar, *Bamboos of India: A Compendium* (Kerala and Beijing, 2002)
Stapleton, Chris, *Bamboos of Bhutan: An Illustrated Guide* (Oxford, 1994)
——, *Bamboos of Nepal: An Illustrated Guide* (Oxford, 1994)
Suzuki, Osamu, and Isao Yoshikawa, *The Bamboo Fences of Japan* (Tokyo, 1988)
Van Trier, Harry, and Jan Oprins, *Bamboo* (Basel, Berlin and Boston, 2002)
Vélez, Simón, Alexander von Vegesack and Mateo Kries, eds, *Grow Your Own House: Simón Vélez and Bamboo Architecture* (Weil am Rhein, 2000)
Villegas, Benjamin, *New Bamboo: Architecture and Design* (Bogotá, 2003)
Villegas, Marcelo, *Tropical Bamboo* (Bogatá, 1993)
Whittaker, Paul, *Hardy Bamboos: Taming the Dragon* (Portland, OR, and Cambridge 2005)
——, *Practical Bamboos: The 50 Best Plants for Screens* (Portland, OR, and London, 2010)
Wong, K. M., *The Bamboos of Peninsular Malaysia* (Malaysia, 1995)
Yoshikawa, Isao, *Building Bamboo Fences* (Tokyo, 2001)
——, Osamu Suzuki, *Bamboo Fences* (Tokyo, 2009)
Yuming, Yang, Hui Chaomao, *China's Bamboo* (Beijing, 2010)
Zhu, S., N. Ma and M. Fu, eds, *A Compendium of Chinese Bamboo* (Nanjing, 1994)

Associations and Websites

WORLD BAMBOO ORGANIZATION
www.worldbamboo.net

INTERNATIONAL NETWORK OF BAMBOO AND RATTAN
www.inbar.int

AMERICAN BAMBOO SOCIETY
www.bamboo.org

BAMBOO OF THE AMERICAS
www.bamboooftheamericas.org

BAMBOO IN MEXICO
www.bambumex.org

BAMBOO SOCIETY OF AUSTRALIA
www.bamboo.org.au

COLOMBIAN BAMBOO SOCIETY
www.maderinsa.com/guadua

ECOPLANET BAMBOO
www.ecoplanetbamboo.net

EUROPEAN BAMBOO SOCIETY
www.bamboosociety.org

BAMBOO CRAFT NETWORK
www.bamboocraft.net

CO2 BAMBU
www.co2bambu.com

BAMBOO WEB
www.bambooweb.info

BAMBOO GARDEN
www.bamboogarden.com

LA BAMBOUSERAIE DE PRAFRANCE
www.bambouseraie.fr

Acknowledgements

One is never alone in the bamboo grove, even among the peaceful silence.

Thank you to Michael Leaman of Reaktion Books for this opportunity.

This book is far from a complete treatise of the immense topic of bamboo, but it is my limited 'attempt to contribute something to the sum of knowledge' of the present bamboo situation, sharing the same sentiment of Isabella Bird in her 1880 book, *Unbeaten Tracks in Japan*. She also went on to write, 'I am painfully conscious of the defects of this volume, but I venture to present it in the hope that, in spite of its demerits, it may be accepted as an honest attempt to describe things as I saw them.'

My sincere appreciation goes to my loving and supportive family: my mother Jane McAdams Lucas, my sister Nancy Lucas Baldwin, nephew Wes, niece Emily and husband Walter Morrison. My father, Frank S. Lucas, would be so proud.

Dear friends tolerate my daily bamboo affliction. I am grateful for the forever friendship of Lucy Morgan Curran, Barbara Browne Gulovsen, Jude Sibley, and Karl Stier, and the hometown camaraderie of all my dear pals in Plymouth.

Thanks go to kind friends for helpful editing assistance: Parker F. Pond, Jr, Cece Crowell, Julie McIntosh Shapiro, Nancy Moore Bess and Elin Noble. Nancy was particularly helpful with information about allegories and folktales!

Many gorgeous photos came through the lens of Noah Bell of Bamboo Gardens in Oregon.

My bamboo network has brought me to marvellous distant lands and into friendly hearts. Immense respect goes to all bamboo researchers; past, present and future.

Photo Acknowledgements

The author and publishers wish to express their thanks to the below sources of illustrative material and/or permission to reproduce it. Some locations uncredited in the captions for reasons of brevity are also given below.

Photo Catherine Ames/BigStockPhoto: p. 128; photo Emily Baldwin: p. 81; photo Bamboo Info Centre: p. 107; photo Karl Bareis: p. 98; photo Bedo/BigStockPhoto: pp. 74-75; photos Noah Bell: pp. 9, 31, 37, 41, 48, 57, 109, 130–31; illustrations by Sally Bensusen: pp. 143, 145; photo Blanchot/Sunset/Rex Features: p. 87; © Gene Blevins/LA *Daily News*/Corbis: p. 108 (foot); © Andrea Bricco/Corbis: p. 116; British Museum, London (photos © The Trustees of the British Museum, London: pp. 8 (top), 18, 42, 44, 46, 68, 93, 96, 97 (foot), 118 (top), 151; photo Chen Wei Seng/BigStockPhoto: p. 70 (top) CHINA SPAN Keren SU/Sunset/Rex Features: p. 21; photo Chris Bicycles: p. 118 (foot); photos James Clever: pp. 32, 55, 126; © Dean Conger/Corbis: p. 122; photo cozyta/BigStockPhoto: p. 8 (foot); photos Ralph Evans: pp. 29, 72; photo Claudio Fanchi: p. 88; HAP/Quirky China News/Rex Features: p. 142; photos Guy Henderieckx: pp. 6, 15; © Fritz Hoffmann/In Pictures/Corbis: pp. 134-135; photos Ned Jaquith: pp. 22, 27, 30, 36, 104 (foot), 108 (top); KeystoneUSA-ZUMA/Rex Features: pp. 65, 147; photo Lalupa: pp. 50–51; photo Daphne Lewis: p. 101 (top); photos Susanne Lewis: pp. 61, 66, 73, 104 (top), 124; photo Liang Zhang/BigStockPhoto: pp. 62, 64; Library of Congress, Washington, DC (Prints and Photographs Division): pp. 17, 71, 139; photos Walter Liese: pp. 26, 103 (foot); photo W. E. Linscomb and the Vermilion Historical Society: p. 47; © Michael Maslan Historic Photographs/CORBIS: 49; photo MOSO International: pp. 112–13; photo Jean E. Norwood: p. 17; © Ocean/Corbis: p. 121; photo Tess Peni/Rex Features: p. 110; © Robertus Pudyanto/Demotix/Corbis: pp. 78–9; photo Christian Rauch: p. 117; photo Razvan-Photography/BigStockPhoto: p. 85; photo rchphoto/BigStockPhoto: p. 69; © Finbarr O'Reilly/Reuters/Corbis: p. 136; photo Kamesh Salam, South Asia Bamboo Foundation: p. 141; photo Robert Saporito: p. 54; photos Julie McIntosh Shapiro: pp. 10, 59, 89; photo Sonja Sheasley: p. 115; photo shiyali/BigStockPhoto: p. 106; photo Shozo Shibata: p. 141; photo Eitan Simanor/Robert Harding/Rex Features: p. 111; photo Karl Stier: p. 58; photo Surf-Skate-Ski/BigStockPhoto:

p. 84; © Tohru Minowa/amanaimages/Corbis: p. 101 (foot); Victoria & Albert Museum, London (photos V&A Images): pp. 20, 52, 97 (top), 114; photo vitalytitov/ BigStockPhoto: p. 67; photo Christina Waitkus: p. 103 (top); photo wuttichok/ BigStockPhoto: p. 70 (foot).

The maps on pp. 33, 34 and 35 are from the Bamboo Phylogeny Group, www. eeob.iastate.edu/research/bamboo; the map on p. 33 was prepared by Brandon Holt and Anna Gardner, the maps on pp. 34 and 35 by Brandon Holt, Elizabeth Vogel and Anna Gardner.

Index